MW00333465

Get Dressed!

Life has stripped you NOW WHAT?

ROZ HUMPHREYS

Crown Me Publications

All rights reserved. No part of this publication may be reproduced, distributed, or transmitted in any form or by any means, including photocopying, recording, or other electronic or mechanical methods, without the prior written permission of the publisher, except in the case of brief quotations embodied in critical reviews and certain other noncommercial uses permitted by copyright law.

Unless otherwise noted, all Scripture references are from the New King James Versions © 1979, 1980, 1982, 1992 Thomas Nelson, Inc.

Copyright © 2015 Roz Humphreys
All rights reserved.

ISBN-10: 0692527990
ISBN-13: 978-0-692-52799-3

The Philosophy of Design

Glenn Parsons

polity

Copyright © Glenn Parsons 2016

The right of Glenn Parsons to be identified as Author of this Work has been asserted in accordance with the UK Copyright, Designs and Patents Act 1988.

First published in 2016 by Polity Press

Polity Press
65 Bridge Street
Cambridge CB2 1UR, UK

Polity Press
350 Main Street
Malden, MA 02148, USA

All rights reserved. Except for the quotation of short passages for the purpose of criticism and review, no part of this publication may be reproduced, stored in a retrieval system, or transmitted, in any form or by any means, electronic, mechanical, photocopying, recording or otherwise, without the prior permission of the publisher.

ISBN-13: 978-0-7456-6388-3
ISBN-13: 978-0-7456-6389-0 (pb)

A catalogue record for this book is available from the British Library.

Library of Congress Cataloging-in-Publication Data

Parsons, Glenn.
  The philosophy of design / Glenn Parsons.
    pages cm
  First published in 2005 by MBI Publishing Company LLC.
  Includes bibliographical references.
    ISBN 978-0-7456-6388-3 (hardback) – ISBN 978-0-7456-6389-0 (pbk.)   1. Design–
Philosophy.   2. Product design–Philosophy.   3. Aesthetics.   I. Title.
  NK1505.P37 2015
  124–dc23
                            2015009425

Typeset in 11 on 13 pt Janson
by Toppan Best-set Premedia Limited
Printed and bound in Great Britain by Clays Ltd, St Ives PLC

The publisher has used its best endeavors to ensure that the URLs for external websites referred to in this book are correct and active at the time of going to press. However, the publisher has no responsibility for the websites and can make no guarantee that a site will remain live or that the content is or will remain appropriate.

Every effort has been made to trace all copyright holders, but if any have been inadvertently overlooked the publisher will be pleased to include any necessary credits in any subsequent reprint or edition.

For further information on Polity, visit our website:
politybooks.com

To William

This one's for you

Contents

Acknowledgements

I would like to thank Dominic Lopes for suggesting this project several years ago, and Emma Hutchinson, Sarah Lambert and Pascal Porcheron of Polity Press for supporting it since. I'm also grateful to several people who took time to read portions of the manuscript or to discuss relevant issues with me, including Andrea Sauchelli, Rafael De Clercq, Larry Shiner, Yuriko Saito, Per Galle, Jane Forsey, Andy Hamilton, Stephen Davies, Allen Carlson, Robert Stecker, Wybo Houkes and the students in my Masters seminar in the Winter of 2014. Two anonymous reviewers also read the manuscript and made innumerable valuable suggestions. Thanks go also to Chris Dragos and Miranda Barbuzzi for excellent research assistance, and to Yuriko Saito for her ongoing encouragement. Finally, I thank my family for their support and patience.

Introduction

There are two kinds of philosophy. One follows the well-trodden paths of philosophical tradition and its greatest minds, taking up perennial questions such as "What is the mind?," "Does God exist?," "What is knowledge?," and so on. In the other, one strikes off from these established paths into wilder territory, and applies a philosophical approach to some hitherto unexplored topic. The present volume falls into the latter category, given that there has not, hitherto, been a branch of philosophy focused on design.

There has, of course, been much *design theory*, and, "philosophy" being as loose a term as it is, this inquiry is often referred to as "philosophy of design." But there is an important distinction between theory and philosophy, despite their overlap. Broadly speaking, the difference is that, unlike philosophy, design theory's primary motivation and focus is the practice of design (Galle 2011). The questions posed by theory are driven and framed by current practical considerations in a way that those of philosophy are not. This by no means diminishes the importance of theory – indeed, for the practicing designer, theory is apt to be a good deal more useful than philosophy. But it does mean that the current body of theoretical writing on design cannot be called a "philosophy of design," in the sense that we can speak, for example, of a "philosophy of art."

This raises the question of what a philosophy of design would consist in, and what good it would be to a student or practitioner of design. Broadly speaking, such a philosophy would examine design, and its specific aims and problems, in light of the fundamental questions that philosophy examines: questions about knowledge, ethics, aesthetics and the nature of reality. It has to be said that philosophy tends to produce a range of plausible positions, each with merits and difficulties, rather than unequivocal results. Also, given their nature, these philosophical positions are sometimes difficult to straightforwardly apply to "real-life" practices. What philosophy does offer to the student or practitioner is a broader perspective on their practice and its relation to the other important dimensions of human life. The ability to see one's daily practice in this way, and to think through its place in the grander scheme of things, is one mark of an educated person, and this is what philosophy can help us to cultivate.

As mentioned, philosophical reflection about the "fine arts," in contrast to design, has a long tradition. In a sense this is understandable, given that we have had works of art for thousands of years, whereas design is a fairly recent phenomenon. Still, design today has a prevalence and prestige that make its neglect by philosophy rather glaring. Indeed, one could argue, amidst recent rumors of the "End of Art," that design today has eclipsed the arts in terms of cultural significance. Be that as it may, it seems clear that the time is ripe for a philosophical consideration of design.

In this book, then, I offer such a consideration, sketching out the terrain for a philosophy of design, and showing that its concerns connect deeply with the sorts of fundamental questions that preoccupy philosophers. Fortunately, this sounds much more ambitious than it is, for two reasons. First, while there has not yet been a distinct field of inquiry called "the philosophy of design," there has been plenty of excellent philosophical work directly on, or relevant to, design by philosophers laboring in various areas such as aesthetics, ethics, epistemology, metaphysics and the philosophy of technology. More than anything else, this book aims to bring this work together into a systematic treatment. Second, we have a template of sorts for such a systematic treatment of design, one left to us by the Modernist movement.

This last point calls for comment, since it is commonplace to dismiss Modernism's philosophical pretentions to be "more than another style," and to see it as precisely that – a rather overbearing stylistic phase that had its day and then passed into the history of Taste. The view taken here is that the Modernists saw, more clearly than anyone else, the central philosophical issues relevant to design, and the connections between them, even if they often failed to develop their philosophical insights. A major element of this book, then, is an attempt to reconstruct key Modernist ideas and subject them to a critical analysis. Although the views that Modernist thinking produced do not always succeed, they remain a vital starting point for a philosophical investigation and I exploit them as such here.

A brief plan of the book is as follows. In chapter 1, I bring the subject matter into focus by examining definitions of "design" offered by design theorists and philosophers. Building upon a definition offered by Greg Bamford, I endorse a conception of design as a particular kind of social practice with its main historical roots in the industrial revolution. In chapter 2, I examine more closely the sort of problem solving that is characteristic of design, and identify an important philosophical problem that arises for it. In this context, chapter 3 introduces Modernism, not primarily as a historical movement, but as a philosophical attempt to address this problem. In the rest of the book, the Modernist response to the problem serves as a touchstone in the discussion of various issues central for design.

In chapter 4, I examine the Modernist's bid to severely curtail the expressive dimension of design, and situate this bid in relation to contemporary thought on the meaning of design and material culture in general. Chapter 5 examines a central concept for Modernism – function – and discusses two philosophical theories that purport to clarify the notion. Chapter 6 turns to matters of beauty and aesthetics, and the Modernist notion that there is a vital relationship between function and beauty. Finally, chapter 7 turns to ethical aspects of design, including design's relation to consumerism, the impact of design upon our ethical frameworks, and possible methodologies for ethical design. I conclude with a comment on the legacy of Modernist thought for our own philosophical investigations of design.

In this attempt to map the terrain, I do not claim to have identified, much less definitively answered, all of the philosophical issues relevant to design. However, I will consider the book worthwhile if it succeeds in showing that design is a realm worthy of philosophical exploration in its own right.

1

What is Design?

When it comes to questions about design, perhaps the most fundamental one of all is simply: "What is it?" One way to respond to
this question would be to pick out examples of design. With a
visit to a design website, or a flip through a design magazine, we
could easily point to some objects that are widely recognized
as products of contemporary design: the Apple iPod, the Eames
chair, Mies van der Rohe's Farnsworth House or Alessi's famous
Juicy Salif citrus juicer. But identifying some examples of design
does not really answer our question in a fully satisfying way. When
we ask "What is design?," we want to understand what makes
the production of these things, and others like them, instances of
design. We would like to discover, in other words, the nature of the
concept rather than mere examples of it. In this chapter, I take up
this challenge, and examine some attempts to define the activity of
design.[1]

Some concepts are hard to understand because the things that
they refer to are unfamiliar: concepts such as God, infinity and the
Big Bang do not correspond in any obvious way to the things we
encounter in daily experience. Thus we struggle to discern their
meaning. When it comes to the concept of design, however, this is
not a difficulty we face. As we will see, with design, we run up
against the opposite problem: the concept of design seems to refer
to too much of what we experience, rather than too little (Heskett
2005, 3–5).

1.1 Defining "Design"

Before we examine some potential definitions of "design," we should first discuss the kind of definition we are seeking. When philosophers attempt to understand a concept, they typically look for a particular sort of definition, which we can call simply a "philosophical definition."[2] This consists of a set of conditions that are individually necessary, and jointly sufficient, for being an instance of the concept. A condition that is *necessary* for being an instance of a concept specifies possession of a feature that any instance of the concept must have. For instance, "being unmarried" is a necessary condition for the concept "bachelor" since to be a bachelor something must be, as a matter of necessity, unmarried. A condition or set of conditions is *sufficient* for being an instance of a concept when anything that satisfies it must be, as a matter of necessity, an instance of the concept. Thus, the conditions "unmarried," "adult human" and "male" are together jointly sufficient for the concept "bachelor," since anything that satisfies these conditions has, of necessity, to be a bachelor. A definition of a concept that specifies a set of conditions that are individually necessary, and jointly sufficient, for being an instance of that concept has the special property of picking out all and only the instances of that concept. In doing so, it provides us with the "essence" of the concept, allowing us to understand it in a particularly satisfying way. Take, for example, the definition of "bachelor" as an unmarried adult male human being. This tells us precisely what bachelorhood consists in, and allows us to understand why any given thing is a bachelor or not one.

In seeking a definition of "design," perhaps the most instinctive thing to do is simply look in the dictionary. But dictionary definitions rarely measure up as definitions in the philosophical sense we have outlined. Take, as an example, the concept of art. We recognize instances of this concept easily enough: performances by symphony orchestras, the paintings of Picasso, the novels of James Joyce, and so on. And we can distinguish these instances of art from things that are not art, such as mailboxes, desks and grocery lists. *The Oxford English Dictionary* defines "the Arts" as "the various branches of creative activity concerned with the production of imaginative designs, sounds, or ideas." This definition is helpful in pointing us in the right direction, but it doesn't capture the essence of the concept. This is because, while the production of imaginative designs, sounds or ideas may be *necessary* for engaging in the arts, it clearly isn't *sufficient*: a politician with an imaginative idea for reforming the city budget, or an engineer who creates a new cooling system for a factory, is not engaging in the arts.

The dictionary tries to reinforce its definition by attaching to it a list of examples: "painting, music, and writing." This list is meant to suggest the distinction that we need here, since it does not include activities such as legislating, accounting and engineering. However, the list, and the definition more generally, offers us no basis for this distinction. Surely there is some *reason* why the imaginative productions of symphonic music are art, and those of accounting are not, but the dictionary definition fails to tell us what this could be. Thus, since it fails to specify a set of conditions that are individually necessary and jointly sufficient for being a work of art – that is, an essence – the dictionary definition does not allow us to fully understand the nature of art in the way a philosophical investigation of it would demand. For these reasons, philosophers interested in understanding the nature of art must move beyond dictionary definitions and work out philosophical definitions of the concept (for an overview of efforts in this area, see Stecker 2003). If, then, we seek to understand the nature of design, this is the project we must also undertake.

The search for philosophical definitions, or "conceptual analysis," as philosophers sometimes call it, is by no means uncontroversial.[3] Some philosophers have been skeptical that such definitions can be found, and this skepticism has been influential in thinking about design (see, e.g., Walker 1989). The philosopher Jane Forsey, for example, rejects the possibility of a philosophical definition, or essence, for design, on the grounds that design is a phenomenon that evolves historically. In her view, this leads to two undesirable consequences. First, any philosophical definition is bound to fail once the phenomenon changes, as it inevitably will. Second, once the definition faces these inevitable counterinstances, the philosopher can only ignore them, "unconcerned with the objects that may then fall by the wayside of his theoretical ambition" (2013, 13).

However, both of Forsey's points are over-stated. The fact that a phenomenon changes does not entail that it changes its essential properties: cars are faster than they were 80 years ago, but this would hardly be a reason to rethink our definition of "automobile."

Second, a philosopher who offers a philosophical definition for some phenomenon need not cling to it no matter what happens in the world around him: he may simply determine that the old concept is no longer in use, and offer a philosophical definition of the new one in play. In short, there is nothing in the historical nature of design to rule out philosophical definition.[4]

With this in mind, let us examine some definitions of design that have been offered by theorists writing on the subject. One important group of definitions is based on the idea that everything we do is design. The design theorist Victor Papanek, for example, wrote, "All men are designers. All that we do, almost all the time, is design" (Papanek 1971, 23; see also Nelson and Stolterman 2012). Design is, in his view, "the primary underlying matrix of life," and includes not only the production of machines, buildings and so on, but even mundane actions such as cleaning your desk drawer and baking a pie. In a similar vein, Henry Petroski says, "Designed things are the means by which we achieve desired ends" (Petroski 2006, 48). This definition includes even natural things that are appropriated by humans, with little or no modification, for use in pursuing some aim. A shell used to scoop water for drinking, for example, counts as a designed object by Petroski's lights. As he puts it, "mere selection for a purpose made [it] designed." On these definitions, designing is understood as nothing more than using things to achieve our aims.[5]

As philosophical definitions, however, these accounts are clearly problematic. Of course, there are some similarities between an everyday process like baking a pie and the process that produced the iPod, the Juicy Salif and the Eames chair. On the other hand, there are also differences, and we do distinguish between the two: it would be strange to call someone who baked a pie a "designer," for example. As a matter of fact, in our everyday thinking we distinguish design from all sorts of other activities in which we use things to achieve our aims: art, science, sports, war, as well as mundane activities such as cleaning and using sticks to draw in the sand. Given that we do make this distinction, we would like to understand the basis for it. But definitions such as "Design is using things to achieve our ends" can offer us no such understanding, since they simply ignore the distinction altogether (Love 2002). Put in more philosophical terms, the problem is that using things to achieve our aims is not sufficient for design.[6]

This raises an interesting question: Why are theorists drawn to this definition of "design" when it seems clearly too broad in scope? One factor here, which I mentioned earlier, is the multiplicity of meaning inherent in the word "design." The word has existed in English for over 500 years, and *The Oxford English Dictionary* lists 16 differing definitions for the English verb alone. One of these is a sense of the word in which "to design" means simply "to intend," as in "When I put up the fence, my design was to give us some privacy."[7] In offering their definitions, theorists like Papanek and Petroski are perhaps drawing on this recognized usage. However, as *The Oxford English Dictionary* indicates, and as my rather stilted example shows, this use of the word is now practically dead: people no longer commonly use "design" in this very broad way (in the example above, most people would probably say simply "I wanted to give us some privacy").

In addition to confusion over different senses of the word "design," however, there may be something else afoot in the proposal of these definitions. One motivation for saying that design is a part of "all that we do, almost all the time," is that this might be seen as a way to emphasize the importance of design. Instead of something done far away, by a small group of specialists, having remote and uncertain effects, these definitions portray design as something all around us. It may then be inferred, from this fact about design, that it has important consequences for all of us and we should pay greater attention to it.

Perhaps this kind of argument is what attracts some theorists to such broad definitions. Certainly, much contemporary writing on design has a polemical quality, explicitly urging closer attention to design. However, as a strategy for achieving this end, the above argument is misguided. Say that, as this argument would have it, design is present in every human action. The fact is that much of what we do is relatively uninteresting and not worthy of serious attention or analysis. To return to some of the previously mentioned examples, cleaning out your desk or using a stick to draw a map in the dirt are not activities that seem to possess any particular significance or call for any special attention. Connecting design to these activities is therefore unlikely to lead to a greater interest in, or regard for, the activity of design (Walker 1989).

If, then, "design," as we typically use the term today, means more than merely using something to achieve a goal, what does it mean?

Endorsements for **GET DRESSED!**

"To be clothed with Christ—spiritually, emotionally and physically is God's heart for every woman. Roz Humphreys shares candidly and powerfully about her own journey towards "Getting Dressed". This book will encourage you to do the same."

Kathy Troccoli—Singer/Speaker

"**GET DRESSED** is a book that every woman regardless of creed, religious beliefs, race or background should read. It is a book that inspires and empowers you to meet yourself where you are at, be it good or bad; and to embrace life's journey. While reading this book I saw myself in many of its pages. I also know what it means to be a control freak and a schedule maniac. I was reminded that I am still a work in progress.

Before I met Roz face to face for the first time, I met her through her writing. I have always been inspired and motivated after reading her blog or postings on Facebook and once again, I find myself taught, inspired and empowered through this book.

If you want to learn what happens when control meets surrender or why at times you need to wear big girls panties, read **GET DRESSED**. You will never be the same and you will become stronger."

Fathima Torres, GEMS Chief Operating Officer

"I read **GET DRESSED** at a time in my life when I was experiencing great depression and uncertainty about my business and life in general. I felt lost and alone, and I felt that there was no where I could turn.

I found it to be very therapeutic and revealing in a spiritual sense. It was like everything I was experiencing - my fears, uncertainties, feelings of inadequacy - were being revealed. It helped me to identify the areas in which I was struggling.

It's very comforting to know that as women of God, it is okay to struggle, but it is not okay to stay there. This book is an invaluable tool that helped me to get through the process, knowing that this too shall pass, and most importantly, that God is in control!"

Donna Hunt, Managing Director HMS Meeting Services

FOR DONNA

Holding Up Your Arms

CONTENTS

Acknowledgements

Thank you to:

My husband Richard. You always said that I would do something great with my writing. I celebrate with you once again, another milestone, with mucho love and gratitude.

My daughters, Kristen and Lindsey. I consider myself super blessed as you challenge me to write as I see it and from the heart.

José and Arcadia Humphreys, the greatest examples a daughter can ever have of Godly parents. Papi y mami, la oración eficaz del justo puede mucho. Estoy muy agradecida.

My sister Brenda for being one of my loudest and greatest cheerleaders. You knew that I could and I did! My brother, José, whose encouraging words resound in my head more often than not.

Titi Maria Adela, you always expected more from me and that has always been my driving force. I continue to strive to become a woman that you can be proud of.

Yvette, Jo, Crystal, Bea, Shari, and Lynn for the constant support and encouragement. Your investment in me is a reflection of what true sisterhood is all about. The life lesson's I've learned from each of you combined and separately are invaluable.

Tim Reid for the partnership for design and cover. You made it easy because of your openness and vision. Wilson a.k.a. Panchito, for your assistance on the final updates. You both rock!

Pastor Frank and Pastor Lisa Santora…your trust and guidance throughout the years are part of life's treasures in my life.

The Faith Church Women's Ministry and Faith Church family. You are continually part of my motivation and inspiration.

Introduction

Each of us has a story, but often strong women won't share the ugly, messy parts. They will share them even less, if they are a leader or a public figure. When I felt the need to share my hysterectomy journey with the girls in my church, I was apprehensive. To be honest, I also thought it silly at first, but as things began to unwind and dive into the negative, the discomfort began to mount. The challenge to remain raw, transparent and unguarded almost sent me over the edge. I questioned whether I shared too much or whether my personal, journal-vomit would help anyone. The response I received took me by surprise.

What finally pushed me to share my story with a wider audience was a visit from one of my favorite artists during my teen years, Kathy Troccoli. She came to our church for her Hope's Alive event. Kathy showcased a new skit that featured her Italian version of the woman at the well. We all loved it. It helped women relate to the biblical story because her conversations were relevant to today's culture. She depicted the transformation that happened in Angie's life in her thick and beautiful, over- exaggerated, Italian accent. That weekend Kathy became the girl next door named Angie who inspired me. After Kathy shared her own heart story and emphasized how important it was to do so, she also convinced me to do the same. I will be forever grateful to her for that.

Three Areas Where Life Can Strip You

There are three areas where life can strip you as a woman.

The first area is physically. Although a woman can sustain most physical challenges (like doubled-over period cramps while maintaining a normal schedule), a series of physical challenges or a devastating diagnosis can strip her physically.

The second area is emotionally. Since it takes mental processing to become emotionally compromised, a woman has the potential to be her worst nightmare. Add outside influences or a catastrophic event and that will surely strip her emotionally.

The third area is spiritually. This has to do with where her core beliefs lie. We all seek spirituality and there are certain events in life that cause a woman to question her core truths and have the potential to strip her spiritually.

These three areas are constantly compromised on their own accord and do not cause a woman to buckle. However, when all three areas are under attack, a woman's armor begins to cascade because the pressure is no longer just from the outside. The pressure is now also growing from within.

In the next few pages, you will read about one of the times where my health was compromised and how this strong woman became stripped emotionally, physically and spiritually. Like anyone else, I had accepted the reality that each of us would be in the thick of our own pain due to illness or loss one day. However, when my one day arrived, I was surprised by how much I wanted to be comforted by another's story. Not just the end-story of triumph but the story in between, the *sandwich portion* of the experience. I wanted to be reassured that the doubts, the frustrations, fears and anger that I felt were valid. I wanted to know that it's okay to feel lonely and that it's normal to feel moments like God is not there, not present.

When you are going through something or are faced with a difficult situation that disarms you, the action to **GET DRESSED** can be as small as a whisper for help, mouthed to heaven. Getting dressed can look like silent tears, heart wrenching cries or surrendered prayer. It's the upward permission to allow God to intervene on your behalf. The wonderful thing is that when you give God permission to intervene, He will meet you where you are.

Self-Evaluation

Intertwined in some of the chapters of this book are self-evaluation sections similar to a workbook that were purposely created to help you:

1. Identify areas you are struggling with or continue to struggle with and have the potential to strip you. It is not enough to read about the experience of another. It is also important to apply what you have learned, but before doing so, you have to unearth all the yucky stuff that you may have experienced or are experiencing.

2. Provide some guidance as to how to get out of a funk without condemnation and to encourage you to **GET DRESSED** again. The last thing you need right now is for someone to tell you to get a grip and snap out of it. However, somewhere down the line, you have to do just that because if you let your emotions lead, you will stay stuck and you will continue to let life pass you by.

You will get out of the self-evaluation sections what you put into them. Honesty, in any self-assessment exercise is encouraged as it will help bring healing and/or correction. Therefore, the outcome will be based on how bad you want a new wardrobe. Your change is up to you.

Where you are right now will be different than where I am or anybody else for that matter. You see, God is a personal God. He is relational and individual. He doesn't want to wait until you get right with Him. He's okay with your asking questions. You can be roaring mad with Him or about a situation. You can feel helpless or hopeless. You can feel undeserving and unworthy. All those things will not stop Him from meeting you exactly where you are, right now, just as you are. Too many of us have been taught that God intervenes based on the number of good deeds one does. That is far from the truth. His intervention is based on your openness towards Him. It's all about relationship...a love relationship.

My expectation is that certain parts of my story will strike a chord, not because you have been through the same thing I have, but because you can relate to my emotions. **GET DRESSED** is your glimpse of how this strong woman acted when faced with pain, illness and loss. It's the place where I tell you, yup, every woman will be unarmed by certain events and most will suffer in silence but you don't have to. You will be pleasantly surprised and relieved to find that we have more in common than you think as I share my yucky, low, high and aha moments.

It's my prayer that my shared-story and the self-evaluation sections encourage you to be real with yourself and others. It is my deepest desire that you find hope in the midst of this tough season of your life; or the courage to conquer, overcome or succeed in whatever next battle comes your way.

The greatest thing about being stripped is that you get to choose how to outfit yourself up again, and it can be done because being stripped…undressed is always temporary. Take heart. You are not alone.

Now, let's **GET DRESSED**!

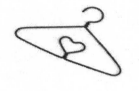

Part I

Bossy with God

ξ ONE ξ
ξ

Being My Best Advocate

WE WERE SCHEDULED for a women's conference and one of my speakers had to back out due to a family emergency. Her topic was about health, and I needed to step in for her. I stripped parts of Lisa Lynn's message and mixed it with my own. Feeling inadequate was an understatement because Lisa was my trainer, and during that time I was being disobedient with my eating. I laughed when I got to the part of healthy eating because by that point, I had chomped about eight small-Snickers (Halloween sized) bites because I was stressed. I remember I told God, I was the wrong person to talk to the topic of health.

Sometimes when God wants to get a point across, He will allow you to get into the line of fire. As I began to unpack Lisa's part of the session for conference, I found that it put me in a tough position. I was going to admonish the gals to keep their appointments but was behind on mine. I had to be transparent and share that I was not following the guidelines for health. We all know that we are a temple, whether we are Christians or not, and it's so easy to eat junk food and avoid exercise. Everything I was about to share, I already knew. Although my intellect was going through an update, I was not following through.

Well, when you are a speaker or teacher, you need to practice what you preach or you're ineffective. Inside I groaned and made a mental note that it was time to make some appointments. What I didn't share was that the month before, my period had laid me out for two days because of a bad ovary. It was time to get the proper attention. I scheduled things like my mammogram and I scheduled a dentist appointment and another with an ENT. Some of the appointments were yearly follow-ups. A couple were because there were things that were ailing me and I kept putting them off.

One of the things I emphasized during the conference was being your best advocate when it comes to your health, and I failed in the breast exam arena. Since I've had cysts in the past, I already knew what an ultrasound with a cyst looks like. After the ultrasound, the technician stated that all was okay. I got up to go change and glanced back at the monitor and noticed two black holes. I groaned and walked away, but what I should have done was stopped and asked. I tortured myself for an entire week. When I finally got a hold of one of the nurses in the GYN office, she explained it was a cyst they had been monitoring that hasn't changed. The picture I saw was in the middle of the waves of the ultrasound. I wish I had asked earlier.

With the next appointment, I was determined to ask all of the questions I needed to. The ultrasound to the ovary came back unsuccessful. They could not see it. Of course my first reaction was how in the world does an ovary become hidden? I was reminded that I had endometriosis and that creates a lot of scar tissue. Now the question I had to get an answer to was: "What's next?", and I didn't like the answer. To remain in my current state was not an option for me. I did not feel comfortable with not knowing what was happening to that ovary. Was there a hidden cyst in the scar tissue? Was there only scar tissue? Was the scar tissue hiding something worse that could potentially kill me? My problems were not limited to the left ovary. They included abnormal bleeding and visits to the GYN every two to three months for over two years.

My doctor gave me three options. Wait for menopause to occur but since all the women on my mother's side had hysterectomies, I had nothing to gauge against as far as menopause age. It could be years before I got there. The second option was to remove the scar tissue around the ovary, but he explained that if he could not see the ovary during the laparoscopic procedure that he would not proceed and would close me right back up. The last option was one I had dismissed for about ten years – a hysterectomy. I politely told him I would think about it. My thought process was short lived because there was an urgency I felt inside to get it done.

When I shared it with a few close friends, the reaction I got was the same. Get it done and get it done fast. However, part of my immediate family was divided. There were valid concerns about the support I would require during my recuperation. It was going to throw off the comfort and rhythm of our home. However, since I had to exercise being my best advocate for my health, I also knew I had to make agreements and arrangements that would bring peace to the entire family. After all arrangements were solidified, I finally reached a place of peace about it and moved forward; but I didn't realize all that would be involved with my decision to have a major surgery.

ξ TWO ξ

ξ

Control Meets Surrender

THERE ARE BLESSINGS THAT COME IN DISGUISES and some that overwhelm you. Right before surgery, there were certain conversations that occurred that would help me through the tough times ahead. Most people would call these coincidences. When I went to Israel, I learned from the tour guide that the word coincidence does not exist in the Hebrew language. Instead they say, as God would have it. One of my best friends had reached out to me. The problem was that we had stopped talking for a while. When I first received Colleen's text, I felt extreme stress as I was not in a position mentally to talk stuff through that had transpired. Also, my emotions were mixed with lots of guilt because I walked away from her after her mom passed. The initial texts were a bit defensive and offensive and I had to stop them because I didn't want to have our long overdue conversation via text. I shut it down by telling her we would meet in the spring after my hysterectomy.

The news of my hysterectomy changed the texts from bad to words filled with love. I made a call to her where I explained what was going on. Not surprisingly, we both said we were sorry and it felt like we never had that break. What did surprise me was that she put me first. She stepped up and was the best friend I needed going into an uncomfortable situation. God knew I needed her and that I would need her even more in the days to come.

My sister was MIA because her job is crazy and she has young children. In spite of this, as I got closer to surgery, her phone calls became more frequent. In one conversation I explained to her that God had formed a shield of protection around me and no harm would come to me. She began to tell me about the story of when she was on a flight for work one day, and how she felt the need to intercede on behalf of my brother and his wife. That intercession was right before my sister-in-law's diagnosis of Lymphoma. As she

21

prayed, she saw linked angels surrounding them in a vision. I always thought of linked as when you put your arm through another person's arm, but her description was that they were standing side by side, leaving no room for anything or anyone to get by them. That conversation helped me better envision God's protection over me. Little did she know how important that description would be in the next few days.

Everyone needs an April. She's the chick that overwhelms you with mushiness. She helps balance me out. She is the gushy person filled with syrupy love and I am not like that. She reminds me that I have to soften up once in a while. When I shared the news with April, she said "Well what can I do?" It's always her first question and usually my answer is nothing, but this time she didn't take no for an answer and I didn't know to what extent she would take it to!

Stuff like a hysterectomy or any surgery for that matter is usually shared with a small number of people, especially when you're one of the leaders in a mega church. However, God had other plans and He started to nudge me to share my journey. Unbeknownst to me, my journey began the year before during the November conference when I was picked to be an example of what it means to be the best advocate for your health, or at least I thought it was limited to that.

On the Sunday before surgery, I decided to post in our women's ministry secret group on Facebook. I explained how my journey began, about surgery and my thoughts, and how I would continue to share my experiences within this journey. I felt naked and exposed but I also felt compelled to be transparent. This was a huge shift for me because we were always taught to be very private growing up, and it was something that my siblings and I took into adulthood. The outpouring of love and gratitude to the posts I shared with the women within our church blew me away. April, the syrupy one, became my point of contact for fielding questions, etc.

I am not one to ask for help. We usually take care of our own and I'm not saying that in a derogatory manner. It's just how we roll within our family. The women's ministry blessed my socks off. I couldn't believe how many wanted to cook and do things for me and my family during my down time.

All of these things were kisses from heaven. The conversations and well wishes smoothed the path for the days ahead.

I am in Control

My husband and I are considered a very active couple. He's a pastor and sometimes together we provide spiritual guidance and mentorships for couples and individuals. I am also the director of the women's ministry. In order to prepare for the possibility of being out for six weeks, I had to organize my home life, my work life and church life. Did I mention I have a full-time job?

With the decision to move forward with the hysterectomy, came the plans to organize, literally, my life. Some people pride themselves in being organized and run a real strict schedule in their lives. I am not talking routine. I'm talking hard-core scheduling that puts regular people to shame. However, I can see where that comes in handy during certain circumstances. I began to take each part of my life and analyze what needed to be systematized via computer or the good old fashion way – paper. I listed out things that needed to get done before surgery and by whom. I listed things I needed to finish or hand off. I listed things I thought I may need to do. I anticipated and questioned what would I do if this and this happened and documented it. I organized documents. I organized schedules. I organized bills. I organized bins, cabinets, etc. I was the organizational queen for a good three weeks.

My biggest disappointment was that when I finally got into the organizational rhythm, it was time to stop and I learned that being a bit on the anal side of being organized actually helped me immensely. It provided me a sense of unexpected peace but it also shined a light in the areas that needed attention. When you have a life like ours, erring on the side of being anal organized is a necessity.

Delegate: *Hand over a task or responsibility to another. (The dictionary forgot to add, without attitude or doubt.)*

I thought that I would have to enlist, okay beg and plead, people to take some of my responsibilities temporarily. What I found was that, for the most part, people volunteered and welcomed the opportunity to step in and help. Of course it was a time of learning for me because, most people won't admit this, but I'm a control freak for certain things. I want them done a certain way by a certain time. What I learned during the exercise to delegate is that you become a better person because of it. You display that you trust the person you hand off to. You duplicate yourself in another and give them the opportunity to grow. You free yourself of unneeded stress.

Delegation of responsibility should be the norm within our lives but women are not very good at it. Our kids don't make the bed right so we make it for them instead of making them do it over until they get it right. We don't ask our spouse for help because they are slow to respond or don't do it the way we want or would do it. We don't ask our colleagues for help because we take their busyness as their inability to learn or perhaps be just as good as us or even better. Let's be honest, sometimes we do not delegate because we want to be the only one to know how to do certain things because it provides value. The problem with that approach is that we forget that we can get sick or drop off the planet without notice and the illusion of being irreplaceable will dissipate fast when someone replaces you.

The other part of delegation is letting go. What that means is the ability and the effort to trust the person you gave your stuff to. That effort requires one not to jump in or want to jump into a situation that may seem out of control. During my leave, I had to apologize to one of my leaders because I felt compelled to jump in to correct a perception on a documented agreement. I should have let her follow the normal path she was heading towards because eventually, she would have found the clarification needed. After my small tantrum and my apology to her, I backed off with the affirmation to her that she had my full support with any decisions she made. One thing I learned and continue to learn is that your body cannot heal correctly if your mind has no reigns on it. Being able to delegate provides a safety on your health regardless.

Surrendered Prayer

Pat on the back I successfully organized most of my life and delegated all of my stuff at home, church and at work. Now I was faced with the daunting questions that had been circling within my mind for weeks; the process of accepting I needed surgery.

During the month of January, our women's ministry goes into a corporate fast. Conversations with my trainer, Lisa Lynn, encouraged me to make some adjustments. I removed coffee from my diet and replaced it with a crud load of green tea. Junk food dwindled to a bare minimum. I wanted to prepare my body for surgery but my mind, my self-talk, was in constant chatter. I rehearsed in my mind what the doctor explained about the risks. I tried to prepare and anticipate what would happen if surgery was done via the caesarean path vs. robotics. It would mean six weeks instead of four weeks and I began to wonder how that would impact everyone and everything I supported. My prayers to God became a dictation.

"God it has to be a robotic surgery, and you said that whatever I ask in your name you will give me." I was guilty of becoming religious for that small span of time because it didn't take very long for me to be corrected. The correction came from a story that one of the guys in my church shared. His wife was pregnant and his prayer was consistent. Let the baby be a boy and he even went into the thank you for the boy mode. His prayer changed when his wife and the baby were in distress during delivery. It changed his prayer from thank you for a boy to all I want is a healthy baby, and He also tacked on the request for God to intervene as best He saw fit. Two days later, one of my leaders shared how she changed her way of praying when something she prayed for did not happen. Instead of getting angry, she surrendered that situation to God and told Him to do whatever He thought was best.

Both of these requests were surrendered prayers. For me a surrendered prayer is when you trust God's way of doing things and for the outcome that He deems best for you. That type of surrender is hard and is not made based on a one day decision. It's impossible to surrender in prayer if you don't have relationship. You can't surrender to someone, to God, if you don't trust them. To trust there has to be a relationship. Both of these individuals had an intimate relationship with God and were able to relinquish to Him during their time of the unknown. They did not know what the outcome would be, but they trusted in God's goodness and knew that all things that come from God are good.

I relinquished my illusion-filled right to dictate to God how I wanted surgery to be. It brought me unexpected peace in my stress-filled mind. However, just because I relinquished that area, it didn't mean that fearful thoughts didn't cross my mind. Like anyone else, the 'what ifs' bombarded me. "What if they found cancer? What if I had to lose one ovary? How long would it take to heal? What if I lost both ovaries?" This is where I had to exercise brain control and not dwell on the unknown. It's easy to get hung up on negative thoughts, but what I've discovered is that some thoughts can rob you of living, quality living.

Part II

Emotional Loss

ξ THREE ξ

ξ

Losing It!

ONE DAY RIGHT BEFORE SURGERY, I became emotional about losing my uterus. Who would have thought? Quite honestly I felt stupid because I had a tubal ligation procedure done years before as we did not want any more children. But now, my ability to carry a child was going to be taken away; no, I was giving someone permission to take that away from me. For a bit there I thought I was nuts. Most fifty year olds do not want to have babies but giving up my ability to do so caused me sadness, like if I was parting with a valuable friend. My emotions and tears took me off guard. I knew I would not be less of a woman because of a missing uterus and quite honestly, I'm not emotional about stuff like that. What was ironic was that the day I went to the GYN for the last consultation, they sat me next to a room where I could hear the heartbeat of a baby in a mother's womb. There are no words to describe what a woman feels when she hears the heartbeat of her unborn child. It pained me even more to know I would never hear that again coming from my belly.

It was a logical decision to have an organ that was no longer of use to be removed especially when it was the cause of so many health issues. My general practitioner echoed my sentiment and even reinforced my decision by telling me that he had seen an increase of uterine cancer in 60 and 70 year olds come through his office, and that I was taking the best course of action. Everything logical patted me on the back but I felt like my womanly emotions were telling me "How dare you!" I didn't get it until, for some reason, the story of Eve popped up in my mind and so to the bible I went because you eventually get that stories don't just randomly come to memory.

Off I went to read something I must have read at least fifty thousand times or more in my lifetime, and I did a double take and read it again. When God told Adam and Eve about the consequence of their sin, God's address only mentioned Eve to Satan. Her and her offspring would always be enemies with him. Before I get more into that piece, if you look at Genesis 3, Satan targeted Eve. Men like to think that it was because she was the weaker vessel and emotional, blah blah blah. However, the reason she was targeted was because he knew that Eve had the ability to procreate in the physical and spiritual realm, and that she also had the vessel to birth in the physical and spiritual realm where Adam did not. If he had targeted Adam, the sin factor could have potentially ended with Adam because although he had the ability to procreate, he did not possess the vessel to birth and pass on the legacy of Satan's plan for mankind.

Now back to Eve. Between the two, Eve was the biggest threat and therefore her being the target was quite strategic. The consequence was that there would be enmity between Satan and her seed. When you have an enemy, they're constantly opposed to you or hostile. Over the years, we have seen some horrific things happen against women. There is sex trafficking, prostitution, genital mutilation, pornography and many things that exploit women, especially towards our young girls. We have seen unequal and unfair treatment, abuse on all levels and the competition game that has become downright cruel. Women's emotions are toyed with and some say that depression may be present twice as much in women than men.

The AHA Moment

The "aha" moment came when I realized that the real reason I wanted my uterus out was because I felt like a target. You may say to yourself but you're always a target and I must agree that is true. However, one mustn't dwell on being a target. I've accepted long ago that when I moved over to the side of Jesus, I became the enemy of Satan and his cohorts. It's a fact of life. You learn that you don't let them know when they've messed with your mojo because you don't want them to take credit. What that means is you keep your complaints to a minimum. Learn to praise even when things get ugly.

Now there are times when you know you're being targeted. It's that spirit check within you. I felt that my uterus had to come out because there was an environment that had been created inside of me that opened the door for a potentially deadly disease. I have way too much I still need to do and I felt it was time to shut that door.

The comfort that came from the 'aha' moment is when I realized how special I am to be a woman. It also came with the realization of how incredible it is that I was chosen to be a woman, because of the unique ability to birth (be it in the physical or spiritual realm). What pisses off the devil is when a woman realizes who she is in Christ, and when she discovers that she can birth dreams and help birth the dreams of others. Even when her ability to birth a physical baby is taken from her, her ability to birth a baby in the spiritual realm can never be. To birth a baby spiritually is not limited to a ministry or a dream that is part of her destiny. As women, we birth encouragement, nurture and love (to name a few) to others on a daily basis. We are a great influence and a power to be reckoned with. Unfortunately, what has happened is that we've been told how we are less than for so long, inside and outside our church walls that we have bought into the lie of the one who opposes us.

God's Bathroom Dance Floor

The morning of the surgery we had to wake up at four in the morning. I woke up a bit earlier to do my hair. One of the gals at work warned me that I would probably have to go curly post-surgery as movement would be limited. When my husband got up, I cranked up the music and danced in my bathroom to *You're an Overcomer* by Mandisa and then to *The Presence of the Lord is Here* by Byron Cage. My husband glanced at me sideways and mentioned it was too early for so much dancing.

In the hospital I began to wonder when I would get the jitters. Four years earlier I had to have a meniscus repaired on one of my knees, and I remembered being extremely nervous. This time, though, there was an unusual calm that enveloped me. The anesthesiologist came in and explained what he would do to prep me, and what he would do during surgery. He then left for a few and when he came back, he told us that he was giving me a sedative and that then my husband could rejoin us. When I felt the hot liquid go into my vein, I remember looking at Rich as my eyes went blurry thinking, the brat anesthesiologist knocked me out and bypassed the sedative. Unlike my last surgery where I sent out lots of prayers before going under, I didn't even have a chance to send any formal ones up and that was okay because I knew God had already heard me. We had wrapped up our conversation earlier on my bathroom, dance floor.

Angel in the Recovery Room

When I woke up in the recovery room, I saw a familiar face. It wasn't my husband. It was one of the gals from my church who was a nurse. Although my brain was in a fog, I knew that she was not on staff at the hospital. I couldn't understand why she was there. I heard her say to the attending nurse, "Take care of her; she's very special to me." Terry came to check up on me later that evening and explained that she used to work at the hospital and had called before my surgery to let them know that I was one of her special friends and that extra care was needed. They allowed her to check on me during recovery. It is one thing to expect to see your husband's face because he's supposed to be there. It's another thing when someone you didn't expect shows up as an example of the physical manifestation of God's love and care towards you. I was beyond touched. Her expression of love towards me kept my peace that first day after surgery.

I have to add that I thank God for my husband because it is his sense of humor that keeps certain situations light. I think he learned that from my family. We are the type that can find humor even at funerals (no disrespect to the dead). When I first woke up, I asked him what happened. I wanted to know if I still had my left ovary or not. He responded with, "The baby is healthy and beautiful and was nine pounds and five ounces and is in the nursery." I responded with a drunk "What????" I asked again, when they settled me into my room, what had happened. He replied, "The doctor was able to repair the knee and you should be up in no time." I kind of gave up after that because it was hard to keep my eyes open.

The doctor later explained that both ovaries were saved and he was able to do the procedure via robotics which meant less healing time.

BEFORE YOU ENTER INTO the first self-evaluation, can I challenge you to become accountable? A commitment takes on more significance when you sign something. It binds you to said document that represents something you become responsible for. In this case, you will be responsible for you. Once you address some of "your stuff," it also becomes your responsibility to help others who may be in a similar situation.

Remember, your level of commitment, your brutal honesty and your willingness to do some soul searching and inventory is what helps you identify, correct and transition you into another level in life.

YOUR Commitment TODAY

I _____
commit to uncovering the areas that need attention and change. I will explore, be honest with myself, find accountability outside of myself (if needed), grow and move forward.

Once I **GET DRESSED** again, I will share and help another woman to do the same because I am called to walk in health physically, emotionally and spiritually and ensure that my sisters are experiencing God's fullness as well...until we all are caught up and returned home.

Dressed as an Incredible Woman

IT IS OKAY TO FEEL and to feel deeply. God gave us emotions for good reasons. When there are sad emotions, it is an indicator that there is a hurt that needs to be addressed. It can only be healed when the depth is acknowledged. When we cut our emotions short, we mask certain things that need to be tended to. Fear to experience emotions is unhealthy as well. It is okay to feel sadness, to be aware of it in life. It is an opportunity to process both emotionally and spiritually so that one can move on in a healthy manner.

During my hysterectomy journey, I had an emotional moment that also made me have an 'aha' moment. (Never discount your emotional, reflective moments. Some of the greatest things can come from them.) The comfort that came from the 'aha' moment is when I realized how special I am to be a woman. It also came with the realization of how incredible it is that I was chosen to be a woman, because of the unique ability to give birth in both the spiritual and physical realms.

Again, we are a great influence and a power to be reckoned with. Unfortunately, what has happened is that we've been told how we are less than for so long that we have bought into the lie of the one who opposes us.

Do you feel like an incredible woman? If not, why?

_____

_____

_____

_____

The bible says a lot of wonderful things about you. Since the bible is God's word, it's safe to say that God says a lot of wonderful things about you. Here are some of my favorites and I have personalized them because that's how God rolls. He's very personal and intimate.

He (God) sings over me. The thought that God sings happily over me fills my heart with joy. Close your eyes and just imagine that for a moment. The God of the universe, your daddy God sings over you. He sings when He thinks of you. If you're a mom, or an aunt, or have babysat, how many times have you sung lovingly over a child? Wow you must be incredibly loved. *Zephaniah 3:17*

My name is tattooed on the palm of His (God's) hand. Although he was referring to Jerusalem, it applies to me also because He loves me just the same. This will resonate real clearly with those of you who have tattooed your initials or your significant other's name on your promise finger.
Isaiah 49:16

I am fearfully and wonderfully made (by God). Every aspect of my body, every curve, all the complexities of my personality were designed to His perfection. I may not like certain things but regardless of how I feel, God loved creating it all. I am unique. You are unique. Nobody else is like you. Nobody can do it, whatever it is, like you. Are you getting an appreciation of you yet? If not, there's more.
Psalm 139:14

I am His (God's) masterpiece. Yea baby! God looks at you and me and He sees one of a kind, priceless, beautiful, magnificent, and gorgeous us. You and I are unique; respectively. *Ephesians 2:10*

With all the negative noise that happens inside and outside of your head, you need to hear the positives about you. However to hear or even read these words are not enough.

What do you really think about yourself at this very moment? Be honest. List it all.

_____

_____

_____

_____

_____

_____

_____

_____

_____

_____

_____

_____

_____

_____

_____

_____

_____

_____

_____

_____

_____

_____

_____

_____

_____

_____

_____

_____

_____

_____

How do you counteract all of those negative things that you believe about yourself? You know the things you may or may not share with others? You change the way you think, and what you say in your head and what you say out loud. It must always be positive no matter how bad you want to say that negative you've been programmed to. What negatives?

I am fat or I am a fatty.
I look disgusting.
I'm not beautiful or pretty enough.
Nobody wants me or who will want me?
I'm not talented enough or I'm not confident.
I won't get the job, the position, the role.
This is a man's world. (No it's not! Girls rule! – Sorry couldn't help myself.)
She's prettier than me. I'm not as beautiful as her.
My butt is too big or I have thunder thighs (ugh).
I can't.

To reprogram you, it will take weeks, months...years. I could apologize again but I won't. This is the harsh truth. You have to conscientiously and purposely stop the negative and replace it with a positive for the rest of your life. This is something that we all struggle with but it's absolutely necessary because if you don't, you will never discover how incredible you are. You attract what you say. If you call out ugly, ugly will follow you. If you call out rejection, rejection will latch on to you like a bad partner. So make a promise to yourself today to start the change.

YOU are an Incredible Woman Plan

If you liked my verses, pick two or three that you will use each time a negative thought or statement escapes from your lips and replace it with that verse. Each time you wake up in the morning, look in the mirror and say that verse over yourself. Personalize it. Each time you're tempted to get down on yourself, talk down to yourself, STOP and repeat those verses.

Write down the verses you will choose to speak about hot and wonderful you.

_____

_____

_____

_____

_____

_____

_____

_____

_____

_____

_____

_____

_____

_____

_____

_____

_____

_____

_____

_____

_____

_____

_____

_____

_____

_____

_____

_____

_____

_____

_____

_____

_____

You are an incredible woman because God says so. In case you're feeling a bit of condemnation and don't feel like you deserve to be talked about so highly, let me remind you that there is nothing that can separate you from the love of God. (Romans 8)

GET DRESSED in knowing that in His eyes you are priceless and He loves you so much that He sent His son Jesus so that He could have a relationship with you. If you haven't experienced God intimately, I encourage you to take the first step and that is to invite Him into your life. That first step will make the rest of your journey here on earth more meaningful and exciting.

ξ FOUR ξ

ξ

Wrong Expectations

MOST WOMEN ARE CONTROL FREAKS. I am guilty of being one of them. I like things to be done a certain way. We live in a pretty decent size house and so the question of upkeep came up and of course my immediate family stepped up. Although both girls were in college, they made a schedule to take turns to come home. My husband stayed with me the first night at the hospital, even though he knew there would be an entourage of nurses coming in periodically. I felt bad but I wouldn't have expected anything less than that from him. A few years earlier, he had a heart attack and that experience changed our lives. We have grown closer over the past few years, and we have learned not to sweat the small stuff. We categorized the small stuff as quite a lot of things that in the past would have bothered us. Our change in perspective helped us minimize certain things to trivial which in turn, helped us get over stuff that probably would have dogged us or given us bad attitudes in the past.

I returned home on a Tuesday and was on the road for an hour because of the pharmacy stop for meds. I began to prepare myself mentally because my arrival meant the beginning of a one-week stay in a bedroom. Although you're released from the hospital a lot sooner than in our parent's days, the same bed rest applies. My sister Brenda and others told me about the importance of following the doctor's instruction and how detrimental it can be to my health if I didn't. When I took the first two painful steps from the garage to the house, I knew that I was in trouble. I had no doubt that I had to be confined to the upstairs portion of the house. The first few days were uncomfortable. Okay I'm being polite. They sucked. Gas and surgical pain do not make for a good combination. The doctors fill your tummy with air when they do these types of procedures. The aftermath blows.

It was hard to get into bed. It was hard to get out of bed. It was hard to find a comfortable position in bed and to make matters worse, I'm allergic to the good painkillers. I was prescribed something that didn't take away the pain, just lessened it. I reminded myself that I had to deal with it and that this was temporary. My youngest daughter came in the next day and slept with me to ensure that I took my meds on time and around the clock. What surprised me, though, is that I felt hurt when my husband went back to the office upon my daughter's arrival. Now here is where I need to add a clarification. My husband is very good to me; nauseatingly so. I chucked it to being emotional because of all I had been through. However, I noticed that my frustration started to increase as I began to nitpick in my own head how things should have been done or not done since I couldn't. The hurt didn't stop there. It began to increase when people I thought closest to me didn't check up on me at all or the way I wanted (sounds selfish… huh).

When you have that much time with yourself and you're confined and in pain, your mind can become a runaway train. Thank God for his grace, mercy, understanding and patience with us. In my hurt, God continued a conversation we started a while before. The following was my take-away when my mind finally got quiet enough to evaluate whether my feelings were valid or not.

Relationships are based on give and take or so we are told. What is not explained is that each of us set an expectation based on our own standards. We measure or define the measurement of what is acceptable reciprocation. The problem that occurs when one uses their own standard is that it becomes a set up for disappointment; sometimes a lifetime of it.

Intimate relationships are complex because it's the melding of two distinct spirits with a supposed common goal… to love each other. However, if the capacity to love is greater in individual #1, which is most likely the case, then individual #2 will fall short whenever the "expectation" of individual #1 is not met. When you understand the capacity of someone's love towards you, meaning what they can provide, it allows for forgiveness and acceptance, instead of resentment and discouragement.

To further simplify, it's unfair to measure your "expectations" against what you believe is enough for you because that other person will always fall short in one area or another. Reality is that they will not love like you although they will try their best to express it. They will not do things like you do or as good as you do, but they try their best. They may never be able to do certain things you want or get anywhere near the mark of your "expectations" but nonetheless they try.

If that is the case, one is constantly presented with a choice. You have the choice to forgive the shortcomings and flaws (just like Jesus does) or you can cultivate hurt and resentment. With that said, can you express your expectations? Absolutely, but after the talk, if some areas do not align the way you want, you will again be faced with the same choice.

I chose to be grateful that my family and my friends tried their best to love me, and that they showed me love based on their capacity and not based on my expectations.

Part III

God's Silence

Where are You...God?

AFTER A WEEK OF JAIL time in the upper level of the house, I was allowed to come down for a visit with one of my favorite cousins. Ed is like a brother to me because we were basically raised together. We have loads of childhood stories and a passionate love for chocolate. He began to share his journey and provided insight into the things that he had learned in the recent year about himself. It made me wonder how much better we would all be if we shared the process, the going through more. I find that each time someone trusts me enough to share the details of their experience, I come away with a different perspective or with a take-away of something that I need to change. Of course his parting advice to me was to rest as much as I could and not to stress. My plan was to do just that or better said continue to.

I began a mild headache that Sunday night after his visit but didn't worry about it because I was going to see my general practitioner for a post-op appointment the next day. I took it real slow the following day and my husband drove me to see him. He noticed that my left ear drum was bulging a little and decided to put me on antibiotics. I explained to him that I had a massive headache a few days before surgery and had gone to the ENT to ensure there was no infection present. His suspicion was that I probably had something cooking that was too small to detect right before surgery. He recommended taking a couple of over-the-counter pain relievers for the continual headache. However, that night was horrible. It was still uncomfortable to sleep from the surgery and the head pain was escalating.

Well I really tried to rest and not stress but now I began to wonder if there was something else seriously wrong with me. Nothing was relieving the pain in my head, so I called my general practitioner that morning. It got so bad that he recommended I go see a neurologist. What concerned me was that before surgery, the ENT had also advised that I needed to see a neurologist. The no stress advice went out the window. I called a neurologist I found in my provider directory and in tears asked if they could see me right away. They had scheduled an appointment for me for the very next day. The next call was to my husband in desperation to get me some migraine medicine ASAP.

When he arrived home with my mother-in-law, I took the over-the-counter migraine medicine and she went Pentecostal over my head in prayer. What is sad is that when she prayed over me, I didn't think God was listening. You see, I'm a leader. I don't need anyone to pray over me. I can pray for myself and believe God for healing. I hope that doesn't come across as arrogant because it isn't meant to be that way. It's just that you learn that in order for you to teach others, you have to practice your own medicine. Right before she had arrived, I cried, pleaded and quoted scriptures over my head. After three days of pain, I went into desperation mode and I couldn't hear or feel God. It threw me into a complete panic and then I became angry. How could God leave me in my most desperate hour of need?

I Will NEVER Leave You

The headache subsided and I could finally get a better night sleep or so I thought. At about three am in the morning I was wide awake and I knew it was conversation time with God. The first question I heard was "Why did you think that I would ever leave you?" I retorted back "Because I couldn't feel or hear you." The reply was the same question. Then the story of Jesus on the cross popped up in my mind, specifically the time when he asked the Father why He forsook him. It is believed by scholars that the Father didn't leave, He just turned away. Now if God didn't leave Jesus when sin was piled up on him, how much less would He leave me, His beloved daughter that has been forgiven? I was reminded of the scripture where Jesus promises never to leave me nor forsake me. I also remembered the scripture when Jesus said blessed are those who have never seen (Him) but believe. It was a humbling experience.

My lesson didn't stop there. For some reason I thought of Lucifer and how horrible it must have been for him to be banished from the presence of Almighty God. Those moments where I felt abandoned by God, I felt lost. I understood Jesus' teachings regarding whomever loves father or mother more than me is not worthy of me. The thought of separation from God was unbearable. It put me in an incredibly miserable state. As I write this, I'm reminded of a dream that I had when I was a teenager. I dreamt that I was walking into the living room of my parent's house but had to go through a hallway. That hallway transformed into a darkish cave that was strewn with demon heads. They were hideous. What caught me by surprise, though, was that my initial state of fear changed quickly to curiosity that made me rattle questions off to them. "What is God like? What is heaven like? It must be beautiful...right?" The more questions I asked, the more their faces became contorted with pain and agony. Those beings will live with the agonized torture of knowing that they will never commune with God again.

Once God convinced me that He hasn't and wasn't going anywhere (I know this may sound silly but I needed that reassurance once again), I was able to rest a bit better for the rest of the day before all hell broke loose.

The next day we had a wicked snow storm and my appointment with the neurologist had been rescheduled for the following day; a Thursday. My brother, José, called that morning and I explained to him what had happened with the headache that didn't want to go away and how God's silence frustrated me. He shared a message he had delivered to his congregation. (Yes, my family has a few ministers.) José shared that he had read that God's silence doesn't equate to His inactivity. For me it was God telling me once again, He was with me.

He then shared the story of Elijah and how God didn't speak to him in the earthquake or in the fire but He used a still small voice. After Elijah was able to quiet himself down, He was able to hear clear instructions from God. Most people think that God doesn't speak unless it's via preacher on the pulpit or by some obvious miracle, but God speaks to us every day. Many times it's that still small voice in your spirit. The way that you know that it is God is because it aligns with scripture. That is the reason why it is so important to learn the bible. The bible becomes a safety net and a rescuer when you need it most.

I would later hear my husband recounting the same story of Elijah to a parishioner on the phone the day before I wrote this chapter. The reminder was two-fold. God reminded me to listen for the still small voice, and it was a reminder that God's silence is actually important in our lives. What comes to mind and best summarizes it is something my pastor, Frank Santora, often says: "Learn to trust God's heart when you can't see His hand." What does that mean? Our daddy God is always working on our behalf, behind the scenes.

Strength Meets Fear

Ten days after my hysterectomy, something went terribly wrong. We had gone upstairs to get ready for bed and my stomach was upset. I started to shake for about a minute and then I felt like I was hit by a hammer on the left side of my head. My hand immediately went up to that side of my skull to cradle it. I noticed that I could not straighten my head. I had to keep my head tilted to the left and my body continued to shake.

My hubs tried to coax me into bed to relax. I heard myself like an outsider tell him "No this is different. You need to take me to the ER." Then I said something that I thought would never come out of my mouth. This scared out-of-her-wits woman told her husband, "I don't want to die." He gave me two aspirins and drove me to the hospital.

My attending physician was a familiar face. She had cared for me other times in the past few years. As I look back now, I saw God's love through my physician. He knew that in my crisis, a familiar face would bring me some calm. They quickly gave me pain medication because I was beyond their pain scale of 10. I was sent for a CT scan. The CT scan came back normal but now she wanted to do a spinal tap. Rich and I gave each other the "oh crap" look.

Both of us did not feel comfortable about a spinal tap procedure being done in an ER. My hubs went into interview mode with the physician about her experience, and when she said she worked in the Jacobi ER (in the Bronx), we both consented. During the tap, I kept repeating "God I know you are with me." I heard my sister's reminder about how I had linked angels around me right before the hysterectomy. I began to imagine the same in the ER. It bought me some level of crazy-peace during a freak-out situation.

Unfortunately, after several tries, the tap was unsuccessful and I was admitted. An x-ray guided spinal tap would be scheduled during normal hospital hours. I was ready to check myself out. My physician was adamant to follow through because there was concern that I may have had a bleed in the brain.

The headache subsided to about a six and I began to text those most important to me to let them know what had happened. (I actually did one text and copied and pasted.) I needed prayer and comfort. My sister came in later that morning right before the doctor arrived, and she heard me tell the doctor, "You need to find out what's wrong with my brain. It's my money maker." My brother called right after the doctor left and my sister recounted what I had said. He reminded us that my sister-in-law, Mayra, had said the same thing when they were about to put a port onto her brain. My heart ached because, even though my head hurt badly, I understood her fear more intimately. The big difference between her and I was that she dealt with a known disease with an unknown future. I was dealing with an unknown ailment with a known future.(At the time, they didn't think anything I had was life threatening.) There is no comparison here, just the realization and a small glimpse of her suffering. It stunk and it was quite humbling.

As I lay alone with my thoughts on the hospital bed, I didn't focus on the why. I focused on others. I thought about how awful it must be for those who spend days, months and years alone with their thoughts and unanswered questions. I thought about how awful it must be for those without faith or hope because although I had both, I still struggled with deep fears.

I remembered my conversation with my brother the day before. We talked about how God's silence doesn't mean inactivity, and I chose to believe that God's hand was at work because I really trusted His heart. You see for me God isn't some made up faith I hang onto during the good. God is someone who is real to me. He has seen me through some really rough spots in life. I didn't think twice about His presence not being there as I had earlier, although the headache I was experiencing was more violent than the one prior during the week. I guess I surrendered my feelings of abandonment and exchanged them for belief. I only got to that place because I had done the freak out and tantrum a couple of days before.

Big Girl Panties

The morning I was supposed to have the tap done, I had a nurse come into my room and explain to me that the exams they wanted to do could not be performed because it was the beginning of the weekend. I would probably have to stay till Monday. That announcement started a flurry of activity within the hospital and with my doctors outside of the hospital. The last thing I wanted to do was stay in a hospital for three more days. My general practitioner was ready to request a transfer to another hospital. I have to be honest. I felt a lot of concern and care from my personal doctors. My general called my husband at least four times and my GYN called to check on me when he heard I had to cancel my appointment to take out my stitches. What doctors do that today? For me their display of genuine concern was like a kiss from heaven when I needed it most. My stress levels were pretty high and hearing both their voices and careful instructions of what they wanted me to do next gave me some ease.

Even though my head hurt, I became my best advocate and advised the medical staff that attended me that I would not wait until Monday and that a spinal tap would need to be done that day or I would request a transfer. A spinal tap was scheduled for later that afternoon. I hardly ate breakfast or lunch and was given Prednisone as a precaution for possible inflammation right before the tap. When we got to the radiology area, I began to feel really nauseous. One of the nurses gave me a barf bag and I wanted to cry and I asked myself "what else can happen?" I began to throw up and that delayed the procedure even longer. When they saw that the vomiting subsided, the radiologist doctor began to explain the process I would undergo. It took a lot of focus.

He wanted me to lie on my stomach. I stopped and reminded him that I had a hysterectomy the week before. They all looked at each other like what should we do now. I had to put on my big girl panties and hold back tears. They suggested I try or they would find another position if it was really uncomfortable. They slowly helped me up to the table onto my stomach and tucked a pillow under it. I dreaded what was next because the failed spinal tap the night before required three different tries. Each time they hit a bone or whatever back there, you get a taste of some sciatic pain that travels down your back side, just not as painful. The doctor began to explain every single step he was doing. I knew the reason but geez some steps I really didn't want to know. When he put the needle in with the Lidocaine, I prayed "God please let him find the spot for the fluid on the first try."

He announced that he was bringing up the table I was on. Picture the head side tilted up in the air and you're feeling like you're going to slide off the table. Apparently spinal fluid can't be suctioned out. One must allow gravity to take its course to retrieve it. Yes the thought "You've got to be kidding me" did cross my mind. By the way the table also moves from side to side and yes, I thought of barfing again. After the retrieval of the fluid, it was explained to me that I would have to slide my body to the gurney after they flipped me around, and that I had to remain flat on my back for six hours. I remembered my earlier question of what else can happen. Crazy as it may sound I asked to see the vials of fluid on my way out. I wanted to see for myself that there was no blood present. They graciously showed me the vials and pointed out how clear each looked. During this whole time, the headache was still at a six on the scale.

Back in my room, flat on my back, the nurse explained I could get up to use the bathroom and eat in two hours and then I would have to be flat on my back again until the six hours was completed. Eating dinner was a challenge because you could not sit at a normal, ninety-degree angle. Flat on my back again, I became very conscientious of the time. Again compassion and empathy began to flood me as I wondered about those who are stuck in a hospital in my current position. I knew my state was temporary but I wondered about those who were in that state permanently or for an extended period of time. I began to pray for them. For many, prayer is a last resort or ditch effort. For me, prayer is the most powerful thing I can do for another.

The room filled up slowly and I found comfort in the familiar faces of my husband, his mother and my daughter. In the minutes that followed, close family friends came to visit. One of them was one of my husband's friends named David. He's a jokester and little did he know that what I needed was to laugh. Anyone that knows me well knows that I love to laugh. My laughter can be obnoxious and embarrassing because it can go up several octaves. I have been threatened in movie theaters by my family. Off David went to the nurses' board in my room and wrote "I will get better fast if my husband visits less...signed Roz." We waited to see if that little statement would raise any reaction from any of the nurses or aides. Not one of them flinched or noticed. If they did, none of them reacted. I laughed when he wrote it and laughed each time a nurse or aide came in.

Yes, flat on my back, I laughed at David's jokes. It made time go faster and once again I was reminded that the fine line between friendship and family can blur. He gave me a dose of one of the best medicines out there...laughter. After everyone had left, my oldest daughter decided to stay with me. I was grateful that the hospital had given me a private room with double beds. As I looked over in the darkness to the silhouette of her form, my eyes filled up with tears. I was reminded of the silhouette of my husband in an uncomfortable bed chair in the last hospital and the silhouette of my youngest daughter, Lindsey, next to me at our home after the hysterectomy. I felt a surge of gratitude for a family that took care of me. It was a reversal of roles and I felt extremely blessed.

DRESSED *in Faith*

GOD WORKS BEST IN THE DARKNESS. You know the places you cannot see; behind the scenes. The hard part is that you have to believe.

When you are in pain, the intensity of the suffering is based on you or how you deal with pain. When you are in pain, it is a place that isolates and toys with your mind and your emotions. It's a place that humbles you. Pain does not have to be physical. It can be deeply emotional. The suffering that pain brings gets more complex when it is a combination of the physical and emotional. All pain will force you to look at your spirituality because, when it comes down to it, that is what you are. You are spirit.

How do you strengthen your faith to know, beyond a shadow of a doubt that God is always there, even when you do not feel Him? You **GET DRESSED** when you read or listen to God's word and then you believe. All of us struggle with areas of unbelief. In there lies the problem. You may struggle with believing for healing physically or emotionally because of something that happened in the past. Perhaps you feel that you're beyond repair and God can't fix you.

What area are you having a tough time believing? What shook your beliefs? Be honest and write out why.

_____

_____

_____

_____

Often, the reason you don't believe is because something in the past tainted your core beliefs. For me, losing my four year old nephew to Leukemia did me in for a few years. I had a tough time believing in healing. It took years of study to finally understand. Years later when my dad had Stage IV prostate cancer, my siblings, our spouses, my mom and I dug in our heels as a family. There is power in a family that is like-minded. There is power in prayer. It is the ultimate power you possess. One of my peeves is when I hear people say, "All I can do is just pray." JUST PRAY! If you only knew that prayer is the most powerful thing you can do! You would pray more often. My dad has been healed for years now. He's 83 as I write this. He's so healthy he still rides his bike for miles in the parks of New York City.

People are afraid to pray bold prayers because they ask themselves, "What if it doesn't happen?" Meanwhile, God is on His throne asking, "What if it does happen?" God's word cannot return empty, null or void because He is the word (1 John 1). Do you believe?

Feeling like God is not there should be temporary. You have to **GET DRESSED** in Faith. Yes, even mustard seed sized-faith. What does that mean? Don't reason with your head. Feel with your spirit. In order for you to believe in anything, you have to study and study and study until you get it deep down into your heart.

YOUR *Faith Plan*

What areas do you think you need to study so that your faith can be strengthened? Look up the scriptures and corresponding stories.

_____

_____

_____

_____

_____

_____

_____

_____

_____

_____

_____

_____

_____

_____

_____

_____

_____

_____

_____

_____

_____

_____

Your next prayer should be to ask God to reveal His unfailing love towards you. The greatest revelation you can have in your life is that God loves you. It's not just empty words. It's a reality that will radically change your life. Once you fall into the chasm of God's love, the expectation of answered prayers changes. Our God is a God of love. He wants the best for you. He wants you healthy. He wants you to be well physically, mentally, emotionally, socially and spiritually. He is a God that is interested and is a proponent of wholeness. He wants you to live a fulfilled life.

Perhaps you struggle and do not believe that God loves you. What is keeping you from believing that God loves you? (Are you comparing God to a man? Did you feel let down by God?)

_____

_____

_____

_____

_____

_____

_____

_____

_____

_____

_____

Here's my challenge to you. I dare you to ask God to reveal His love towards you. Say it exactly like this…"God, let me see how much you truly love me." He will meet you where you are, right now, just as you are.

My Prayer is That He Overwhelms You.

Sometimes we find prayer to be a chore because we repeat the same thing over and over again, because it has become a rehearsed complaint, or because it has become a string of words that one feels must be religiously said. Now put yourself in God's shoes. How would you feel if somebody talked to you like that every day? I have full blown conversations with God. I dare say I talk His ear off at times. I'm a woman. I can't help it! However, I do understand the importance of praying the word; the bible. When I am sick, I find verses and I put my name in those verses. I remind God of what His word says. Bold huh? You got that right! You are the daughter of the Most High God. He wouldn't want it any other way.

Practice conversing with God. Get the verses for your situation (Google is a beautiful thing), and speak them over your current situation. Write those verses below and personalize them. (Example: Thank you God because I can do ALL things through Christ who gives me strength. Philippians 4:13 -paraphrased.)

_____

_____

_____

_____

_____

_____

_____

My sister-in-love, Mayra, used to talk about finding and following the light when she was in the horrid process of being chemically healed after being diagnosed with Stage IV Lymphoma. When you are thrust into the darkness of an illness or any adverse circumstance, the light is what causes you to overcome. Many will view the overcome part as the victory over illness or that adverse circumstance. I think that's a small part of it. This is my opinion. I believe that the pathway to the light is that place where you can let go of cynicism and embrace comfort, most importantly God's comfort. When you know how much God loves you, truly and dearly loves you, like Romans 8 loves you (your hint to go read), His light becomes your path.

GET DRESSED with the comfort and the knowledge that God is always with you. Let it become a tangible reality that nothing and no one can shake.

ξ SIX ξ

ξ

Why Me?

THE HEADACHE FINALLY SUBSIDED and the hospital advised that the spinal tap came back normal. When I asked what caused it, no one had an answer. They advised that I should follow up with a neurologist. At that point I just wanted to go home. Twice in a hospital in two weeks had worn me down emotionally. When I got home, I felt beat up mentally. The absence of a bad headache meant that my mind began to swirl with unanswered questions. "What if they missed something? What if I have something that is life threatening?" It was Saturday and I couldn't call the neurologist's office to make an appointment. The thought that I had to wait began to stress me out.

Later that evening my husband's cousin, Wilson, came for a visit with his wife and my goddaughter. They had delayed seeing me because they had some bug going through the house. Most people would want silence but at that point I wanted and needed the distraction. I explained to them both what had happened and how I felt. This was family and I didn't have to put on my bravery hat with a parishioner. I think that is the mistake most people in church leadership do. They don't allow for vulnerable moments in front of those they lead. I've noticed lately that I've stopped that for the most part, and if I am having a crappy day I usually just say it's not a good day or just answer okay when asked. I don't go into details with everyone because that's not wise either. However, in this case, it was family and close family. We had gone through some rough spots in the past with them and I welcomed the comfort of being myself.

The Unknown

The guys left to get pizza and I stayed behind with Iris. She was my therapy and didn't know it until I told her a few days later. She sat and listened. I had to sort through a lot of emotions and it was easier

71

for me to explain it to her because she was a woman. Even though she had never gone through what I was experiencing, she could relate to the range of emotions that I was going through. She empathized and didn't give me sympathy. I didn't want sympathy. I wanted someone to listen and acknowledge that I was hurting in more ways than one. She listened. I shared about my fears and my fears were very real. At no time did she diminish what I felt or make light of it. Here I was at home and I was going to be alone soon and I had valid fears. "What if the headache came back and I was alone? Should I be alone? How long is this going to last? What if the neurologist finds something?"

These questions may sound like a lack of faith or some people would interpret it that way. Perhaps at that moment it was true or perhaps it was a moment of complete vulnerability. I think often times we become too spiritual, and we forget that we were created to feel. Those emotions were placed there quite purposely. I had to go through the process of fear of the unknown. It was normal. It sucked too. It put me in a very vulnerable and lonely place. No matter how surrounded I was by family and friends that loved me, I felt compromised emotionally and I did not like it. Remember I am the woman who likes to have control of her world, and this whole thing reminded me that control is an illusion that we neatly package with a bow. When it gets disturbed, it creates a bit of chaos.

I had to work through the chaos of unanswered questions that would not have an answer for days or perhaps even weeks. I excused myself from my family and made a call to one of the pastor's wives in my church that happened to work at the neurologist's office. Again, there is no coincidence. I explained to Donna what had happened and she began to alleviate some of the stress that I was experiencing. She assured me that she would check on Monday morning for appointments that week. Her temporary partnership with me alleviated some of the real fears that night. The partnership of my family that visited did the same.

A Kiss in the Box

The neurologist was scheduled for a Friday—one week and one day after the massive headache. The wait was a bit torturous because I had mild headaches that continued throughout the week. What I discovered was that it was okay to sort through all of my raw emotions and acknowledge them. To hide them would do me no justice or help. Once I got to the point of okay this is how I feel, I had to figure out what I was going to do about it. You can only sit in your poop for so long. (That is what my friend April says.) I have to admit, I didn't run to scripture. It's hard to focus when your brain hurts and when you have that much clutter in it. I did run to God, my constant. During this whole time, my chatter with Him had been constant. I really did talk His ear off so my sorting of emotions wasn't just with family.

The neurologist visit was after yet another major snowstorm. We got pounded with snow and it felt more like living in Alaska. The appointment time had to be changed because we had such a hard time getting out of the vicinity I live in. Even with the time change, I still made it late. When I got there, all appointments were behind. I did not complain. I waited patiently because I wanted this over and done with. He scheduled me for an MRI because he found that the spinal tap had actually uncovered that I had a mild form of meningitis. The hospital failed to mention that.

I was surprised by how fast the insurance approved it. The radiologist department called the same day to let me know they had a slot open for the upcoming Monday morning first thing at 7:30 a.m. The quick turnaround made my brain go into a spin of more questions and I had to yell at myself to get a grip as it was being done to disapprove anything serious. Yet in the back of my mind, I had that nagging thought of what if they uncover something hidden?

In the MRI box, I had to chuckle because this thing makes computerized sounds and tapping. I began to wonder what they would do if someone had a bad headache because that thing would make it worse. To alleviate my fears of being in a confined space with a contraption that was locked above my face that looked like a hockey mask with big spaces, I began to imagine the angels once again. This time they were linked around that MRI machine and linked outside my door. I imagined that if any spirit would walk by, they would guess there was one of God's favored daughters in the room who is being heavily guarded. The best part was when I saw God lean over into the machine and kiss me on the forehead. That part of my imagination was unexpected. It was a loving reminder that I was not alone in that box. It was my greatest comfort.

I asked the technician to throw on some Christian Contemporary music and the one song that stood out the most was *Stronger* by Mandisa. I guess it resonated with me because I've learned more in the past four weeks than I would probably learn in the entire year. Later that afternoon, a headache came on and I didn't mention it to my husband until almost 9 pm that night. I caved in and took the migraine medication prescribed to me. This was done with frustration and the knowledge that the headache may have been due to the dye for contrast done earlier that day during the MRI.

Why Me?

My return date to work would soon be upon me and I needed to know if I needed an extension to my medical leave. I called the neurologist office and they confirmed that the preliminary MRI results looked good. Instead of being happy and relieved, I found myself completely irritated, and yes that included irritation with God. Questions like "Why did you let me go through this? What was the point?" went through my head. The more I thought about it, the more irritated I became. I decided to bring my thoughts of irritation to my husband. I asked him "Why me?" and he replied "Why not?" The thought of hitting him did cross my mind. He asked me to answer his why not question. One of the first things I blurted out before I could catch myself was "Well I am the daughter of the Most High God and these things shouldn't happen to me." He replied again, "Why not?" I answered, "Because these things should not happen to me. I should be protected." He replied, "Why not?" The more I answered, the more irritable I became because eventually, I answered my own question.

Perhaps you thought it arrogant of me to answer the way I did. As I look back I must admit I would probably think the same but my answers weren't driven by arrogance. (Okay maybe a little.) They were based on the knowing of who I was. There were certain expectations that I have because of it. As crazy as it sounds, it would have been easier for me to accept that they found something in the MRI because then it was being addressed. MRIs reveal things that are hidden from normal tests. The fact that I had nothing made me mad because I went through all these tests that scared the crap out of me and all turned out to be fine. I should be happy right? What peeved me was when I realized that this whole thing was a vicious attack by the enemy and I felt unprotected. The realization caused me a substantial amount of irritation.

As I began to sort through my irritation with my husband, his final reply shut me up. He explained that sometimes God allows certain things to happen because He wants to stretch us and our faith a little bit more. You always grow from these types of experiences. I let out a long sigh because I knew he was right. I also knew that my irritation was irrational. Some of us think that we should be exempt from any of the ugly stuff that happens in this world. The reality is that none of us are.

A few weeks before the surgery, I had picked up the book *Have Heart* by Steve and Sarah Berger and began to read it for a second time. I didn't understand why but during this irrational moment, what came to memory was something that comforted Sarah and brought great meaning to me. The book is about the loss of her 19 year old son and how real heaven became to them. One day the Lord told her "Josiah just lives in another country." She replied "Whose builder and maker is God" (Hebrews 11:10, 16)[1]. The realization that I was not from this country hit me with full force. Let me explain.

I am the daughter of the Most High God. My country is heaven. Although I live on this planet, within this hemisphere and realm, this is not my permanent home. I live in hostile territory and when I became God's daughter, I was given certain territory to defend. This territory was taken from the enemy and given to me in the spirit realm.

Many people only see the property surrounding my home, but in the spirit realm, my reach of influence goes much wider.

> Each time I pray for myself, for those I love and others who ask for prayer, that influence goes wider.

> Each time a life changes because of me, that influence goes wider.

> Each time a miracle happens in a person's life and I contributed to it somehow, that influence goes wider.

The wider my spiritual influence or territory goes, the more irritated I make the enemy because I continue to take away from him. I am not in my country. I am in enemy territory and my mission is to get my daddy's kids back into His kingdom and in the process, I not only take back spiritual realms, but places and resources that were supposed to be mine anyway.

This reminds me of the children of Israel. For their entire existence, they've battled to keep what is theirs. They have stood their ground in their beliefs and for their land. They have fought enemies their entire lifetime. Why should I be any different?

ξ

DRESSED *in Trust*

IT IS EASY TO FALL INTO that "Why me?" victim mentality. You probably have asked God at one point or another: "Why did this happen to me?" There will be some answers that will not be given to you until you pass on over to the other side. I know that's probably not the answer you want to hear, but you have a choice. Stay in the misery of asking why or trust that God has taken all of the pieces of your life and He has turned the yucky stuff around for your good. (Romans 8:28) Attitude is a choice. Response is a choice. You can live in misery and continue to look at what you've missed or how you been wronged, or you can let it go.

The answer to my why me question from my husband really annoyed me, so now it's my turn to annoy you. Why not you?

_____

_____

_____

_____

_____

_____

_____

_____

You probably didn't like that exercise. I didn't either. Perhaps you wrote things like, because I am a good person; or because I am a child of God; or these things shouldn't happen to me.

The reality is that there is an enemy. You may choose not to believe that, but it doesn't change the fact that He's out there with whole lot of help and their mission is to take you out...literally. It's a sobering fact.

I know how hard it is to let go of the why me? After my short tantrum with God, there was the reminder that I am not exempt and that I live in a broken world. What that means is that negative stuff will happen during my lifetime. However, I believe I will always be under God's protection. One day I will know the 'what' God protected me from. I remind myself that the illness after my surgery could have been a lot worse and perhaps God blocked it.

To believe that, there has to be a high level of trust and in this case, trust in God. If you don't trust, you will constantly question the why of any and every situation. This can cause you to live a life of unrest and worst, of misery. To trust there has to be a relationship. If you don't have a relationship with God, you cannot trust Him. In the prior evaluation section, I encouraged you to have conversations with God. In this section, I encourage you to study how to trust God. Study until you have the 'aha' moment and there's nothing that can change your mind otherwise.

Often I remind women that God is not a man. (Numbers 23:19) What that means is that you should not compare God to that man who hurt or betrayed you, who continually disappoints you or that man who continues to abuse you. He's not that man that did not keep his word, who broke all his promises or never came back. He's not the missing or absentee dad or the neglectful husband or father. He cannot do any of those things because it goes against His nature. He can be trusted.

YOUR *Trust Plan*

It's not enough to believe that there is a God and then reach out only when there is a crisis. In order for you to reach a place of peace, you need to hand yourself over to God and trust that He's got you.

What are some of the areas that you're still asking why me and have not handed over to God?

_____

_____

_____

_____

_____

_____

_____

_____

_____

_____

_____

_____

_____

_____

Once you give it to God, don't take it back. Okay, just a word of warning. You're going to take it back because you're probably like me, a control freak. It will be a back and forth game for a bit, but then you eventually figure out that you can't fix it so what's the point of trying to. There are just certain things in life that need divine intervention. Once you stop trying to solve or fix it, wait. I can see your eyes rolling because I do the same thing when I hear the wait word. You have a choice. Delay the answer because of your meddling or receive the best answer. The best answer is worth the wait. During the wait, when life happens, because it will happen, learn to keep the why me to a minimum and trust that God will use everything in your life, including the bad and ugly, and turn it around for your good (Romans 8:28). One day you and I will find out the why.

In the meantime…**GET DRESSED** in Trust.

Part IV

Aftermath

ξ SEVEN ξ

ξ

Raw & Vulnerable?

WHAT CAUGHT ME BY SURPRISE was the overload on my emotions. The third and fourth weeks after the hysterectomy were brutal. I experienced delayed reactions and I guess everything caught up with me in the aftermath. I blubbered with every sappy commercial or movie or just because and it annoyed me to no end. I would yell at myself, "Woman, get a grip" but that wouldn't help. Instead of being kind to myself, I was harsh with my mind and said words like "buck up" or "cut it out," None of these phrases seem to take effect. My emotions just went their own way and I couldn't pull the reigns hard enough to bring them back to where they needed to be.

The reason I'm so tough on myself is because I wanted to avoid falling into depression and I considered myself a strong woman. When you've experienced depression and it has kicked your butt, you try to your best not to allow for it to rule or reign in your life ever again. If you've ever been in that dark, deep pit, you know that to allow yourself to get back in there is not an option. The problem though is that you can become so rigid that you forget to allow yourself to feel anything negative. You can actually condition yourself to shut down negative emotions fast and avoid feelings. Although that type of shut down is not entirely bad, it's not entirely good either because sometimes your emotions are so rattled that they need some type of release. That release can come through processing it with a friend or just having one good cry or 20. I didn't like the 20 part. I began to wonder if there was something wrong with me.

What I recognized is that I am good at internalizing my stress, sadness, grief, disappointments, discouragements, etc. I come from a family of strong women and control is mandatory especially if you have to be strong for others. Being a strong woman was ingrained in our family, and we took that to all areas of our lives. The problem with being a strong woman is that people seem to think you always have it together and that you're one tough girlie all of the time and that is far from the truth. A strong woman usually is a chick that has learned to put herself to the side to meet the needs of others first. By the time she's finished, the next person or project has rolled along and the stuff she wanted to scream or cry about is still there but she doesn't have time to succumb to feelings. This vicious cycle usually works until something traumatic or extremely painful happens.

In my case, I had delegated everything, even housework, and all of the sudden I had all the time in the world to face an entourage of emotions that I would have otherwise kept in check on a normal, busy, schedule. So here I was faced with the battle to maintain my strong woman status that did not want to succumb to depression. Yes it was awful.

What finally did me completely in was when one of the girls in my women's group went home to be with Jesus and I found out via Facebook. Many people criticize Facebook but I actually like it because it has helped me to reconnect with old friends and it has provided an easy medium for me to communicate my writing, as well as to keep engaged with updates on family/friends and activities within our church.

My sweet Sue would comment on a few of my posts in FB and I considered her one of my greatest cheerleaders. She had a few health issues but she had always beat the odds. One day in the midst of my bouts of tears, I noticed that Sue hadn't been posting anything. My posts were far and few during that time so I didn't notice earlier that she had gone missing.

As a leader, I began to beat myself up mercilessly that I hadn't checked on her earlier, etc. She passed quietly and I felt so bad that I didn't say goodbye. God reminded me that I had bumped into her right before surgery and her parting words were I love you. As a matter of fact, she said it three times. The last time as I turned to walk away she said "Hey Roz, you know that I really do love you." It brought me comfort because unbeknown to both of us, Sue had actually said goodbye and knew that I loved her too.

Depression's Grasp

I thought of doing an edit on the following to change it to past tense, but decided to leave this part of my journal entry as is. I believe it will help some of you to understand and know that you're not alone.

Journal

There's an ugly-dark monster that has reared its head. He's foreboding. I compare him to the dark side of Mr. Clean. He towers over me and the cast of his shadow is long. Once again, I tell myself it's just a shadow but the fight has been fierce. Days like today I feel like I'm on the losing plain. My heart grows heavy with sadness because I failed. I succumb to all of the emotions and darkness threatens to swallow me. My emotions range from irritation, to disgust (with myself) for allowing it—depression—to control me. I am then thrown into utter despair because I see no rescue and no way out. I know what to do and yet I find that I cannot do it or I am slow-moving towards the light. I always seek the light because where there is light, darkness cannot abide, no matter what shape it comes in.

I go internet happy, read and discover that even though my ovaries were not removed, there is the possibility that the vehicles that supply blood may have been injured or compromised. This means hormone fluctuations that cause all sorts of emotional chaos. A long sigh escapes me and I wonder once again where is the light, the end of this crazy ride I took for the sake of my well-being. I acknowledge that I don't like people very much and have pity on the man that lives with me.

I consider myself blessed not to have had all the other side effects that I have either read about or have been told about by countless women but nothing has prepared me for the onslaught of irrational emotions that I'm experiencing.

This control freak, strong woman has lost her grip and, obviously, all the efforts to pull out of this ain't working. Yes I used the word ain't. So, you're probably wondering what the game plan should be now. Several steps have crossed my mind as I write. I have started some. Others I will need to do. The obvious was the sit down with my other half to explain why his loving wife has been riding the broom lately.

The next thing I did was a bit difficult for me. I enlisted the support of gals I trust and that wouldn't be shocked to learn that I am as human as the next gal with perimenopause on steroids. Now I have to admit I've been talking to God but the past couple of days have been more like griping and complaining "Why did you make me a woman?" sessions. And God, you have to love Him, points out how magnificent the woman's body is. Being the ungrateful daughter that I am at the moment, you can understand why I am not in a very appreciative mood.

I have to say I am mortified by my honesty but perhaps that is what is needed at our womanly tables. We sugar coat how we feel and don't say it like it is. We hide our hurts and pain with smiles and laughter and lie through our teeth each time we're asked how we truly are. Truth be told, here's where the balance comes into question. Of course I don't believe we should tell everyone our problems or our pities but there must be a balance. There has to be a place of trust where we have gals in our lives that love us enough to be sounding boards from time to time. Otherwise, how do we get through?

I don't believe in dwelling on problems because there will always be a problem. However, I do believe that something is required of me as an individual. Often you and I stay stuck because we take no action. We pray and expect something miraculous and although I believe in prayer and miracles, I also know what God expects of me. He expects me to make good and healthy choices. He expects me to let Him know about the good, the bad and the real ugly. He expects me to get help when I need it from others because we were created to be social beings. Isolation is against His nature and His plan for us.

My girlfriend Jo pushed me to write because she knows this is my therapy especially when my mind is jumbled or troubled. Writing soothes my heart, my emotions and my soul. It also puts a smile on my God's face. My actions were many and very strategic in this case so that I could grope in the darkness until I found the path to the light. Each time I acted, I could see the light become brighter at the end of this dark tunnel called depression. To ignore it is not an option. To succumb to it is not even a topic of discussion or even negotiation. I admit I struggle but I will continue to battle towards balance and my well-being.

To overcome this imbalance, I know the changes I have to continue to make. Eat healthy, exercise, surround myself with good friends, don't isolate, put up my sticky notes with verses and positive statements, fast, pray and trust that my knight in shining armor (Jesus) will come to the rescue – much sooner than later. These are my proven steps from times past.

You may wonder what I will do when I feel my lowest and feel like I'm beginning to spiral into that dark pit. I will repeat all these proven steps because they worked for me. They worked before. They will work again. To be honest, just writing about it made me feel better…a lot better. I see the light.

Self-Evaluation

ξ

Dressing Requires Action

DID YOU EVER FEEL raw and vulnerable? What caught me by surprise was the overload on my emotions. The third and fourth weeks after the hysterectomy were brutal. My emotions just went their own way and I couldn't pull the reigns hard enough to bring them back to where they needed to be.

I had to question if what I was experiencing was sadness or depression. I really had nothing to be sad about. I was happy my uterus was gone! The emotions I was feeling were overwhelming. There was deep hurt and I couldn't pinpoint why. I felt sad all the time. One can experience deep sadness that is prolonged. An example is grief.

What makes you feel raw and vulnerable at this moment? Why?

_____

_____

_____

_____

_____

_____

_____

I knew I was slipping into depression. I was raw. I was vulnerable and I was scared. What I was experiencing was not clinical depression. My heart aches for the women who experience that. Often people do not understand or realize that there are different levels of depression. Sadness is one of the many symptoms of depression. It's very real and women in the church do experience it.

To know the signs of the onset is important. It can easily creep up, for example, because of a break up. (I was tempted to say a bad break up but I've never seen a good one.) It can appear after the loss of a loved one. It doesn't matter if they were ill or taken suddenly. It can overcome you when you've been ill for a very long time or you've been given a short time to live. It can come with the seasons. It is usually subtle and builds over time. By the time you realize you're in the thick of it, you've been there perhaps for weeks or months.

Silence is one of depression's friends. Isolation is depression's soul mate. Distortion of thoughts and how one processes and reasons becomes depression's faithful companion. It takes A LOT of effort to reprogram because there's no energy. It's been zapped. Everything becomes a chore and your bed looks like the safe haven for the jumble chaos you feel. You feel hopeless, helpless, worthless and even guilty. The physical symptoms can include stomach and body aches. Forget about being able to make decisions.

Do you think you are depressed or just very sad? If so, why and what caused it?

_____

_____

_____

_____

_____

_____

What I found is that fear and depression go hand in hand. Fear can make the struggle worse than it really is or can be, because fear is fueled by unfounded realities. It fills your head with the "what ifs." Fear will gladly take the lead. Think about it, many of us gals have been conditioned to believe that fear keeps us safe, that fear creates boundaries and that fear is what protects us. It's a lie that keeps many captive within certain areas of the mind, emotions and heart.

It takes courage to face whatever it is that fills your heart with dread. It can be the acknowledgement of something that occurred in the past. It can be letting go of something or someone. It could be venturing into the known or being faced with the unknown. It could be about something real or something that is made up in your head. I heard that most of the things we worry about never happen.

Are there areas in your life where fear is keeping you paralyzed and unable to move forward? Why do you think you can't get passed it?

_____

_____

_____

_____

_____

_____

_____

_____

_____

In today's world, we use the word sad and depressed interchangeably. Instead of saying that we're sad, we choose the word depressed instead. It somehow gives it a more in-depth description that warrants the attention of others. You get more concern from someone if you say you're depressed instead of sad. The answer to sad is usually, you'll get over it, whereas the response to being depressed would probably introduce solace and conversation.

People say you are what you eat. *I say you are what you speak.* Unbeknownst to you, each time you say you're depressed, you welcome the spirit of depression. Your words have weight in the spirit realm. There is a universal law, whether you are a Christian or not. You attract what you want.

How do you communicate what you want? You speak it. Look at your life. You will notice that whenever you were excited about something that was going to occur, it happened exactly as you spoke about it. However, if you felt dread, discouragement or negativity about something, the outcome was exactly that. Ever wonder why someone in the same adverse situation as another, has a positive outcome whereas the other doesn't? It's because of their self-talk inside of them as well as outside.

What is your self-talk like? How do you respond when someone asks you how are you doing when you're sad? Would you say you're more positive or negative, and why?

_____

_____

_____

_____

_____

_____

You may be wondering how I recovered from my bout of depression. I did several things. Years ago, when I had experienced it, I put into practice the following things that worked for me. Although I didn't need a therapist or medication this go round, I did repeat the same exact steps that helped me get out of the depression pit. It took a lot of work. There is no easy in this because you don't feel like it. In the beginning, it's mechanical. The steps below will work for any circumstance by the way, and does not have to be used just as a way out of depression.

I surrounded myself with two to three friends that I could be accountable to and that I trusted. Contrary to popular belief, leaders do become sad and depressed. Pinch us. We feel.

Junk food had to be cleared out and I had to load up on healthy foods. (My trainer Lisa says she can't hear God when she's not eating clean.)

I had to push myself to move the body and get the heart pumping. Exercise is not the activity that is on the top of my list, but there are benefits it brings, like good endorphins that put you in a better mood.

Post-it notes became my best friend. Since I was combating a lot of negative thoughts, I had to have visuals of positive ones. This meant putting post-it notes EVERYWHERE with positive statements or verses.

Music is the soother of the soul. Happy, Latin music is a Puerto Rican's invitation to, at minimum, a sway. When you're in a funk, even a sway is a good thing. My favorite though, is worship music because it gently and instantly transports me to the throne room…my greatest comfort.

Praying; it's not repetitive or boring. It's conversation. Yup, you know already. I talked God's ear off some more. By the way, when you're depressed or sad, tears are the loudest prayers.

I reminded myself to be grateful. When the mind is clouded, it's easy to forget to be grateful. At night, writing down three to five things to be grateful for within that day changes perspective.

One of my greatest outlets is to write. Often when I speak to women who are confused, depressed or sad, I ask them if they journal. What that does is that it removes all the stuff that's circling in their head onto paper. Journaling relieves the stress of the constant analyzing that we all do as women.

These proven steps can be applied to most any situation. To **GET DRESSED** again requires that you proactively find positive ways to get out of a negative situation, even if it means just emotionally. You may not be able to fix the illness that is in your body or the bad relationship you're in right now, but your attitude can become a positive one as you expectantly wait for healing or restoration. Again, there is no easy. It takes work, a lot of it sometimes and persistence. The reason some women don't heal, is because they don't like the price tag. It's too high.

What is your plan to get past that struggle within your life? Maybe it's not prolonged sadness or depression but it's something that happened in the past or in the present. You have found that you cannot move forward. It's time to **GET DRESSED**. Make the following plan and stick with it.

YOUR *Action Plan*

Surround yourself with a couple of girlfriends that you trust and that you can become accountable to. They have to be trusted friends and not acquaintances. They cannot be going through what you're going through now. These gals should be known for speaking the truth you need to hear but who love you enough to be gentle when considered necessary and tough when you need it too. Why do you need girlfriends? They will ensure you stick with your plan.

List the two girlfriends you will enlist, if you haven't done so already.

_____

_____

Health is an important part of life. It is not limited to just healthy food and exercise. It includes keeping your medical wellness checkups. It saddens me when women put themselves in the backburner because I've lost friends because of that. I was guilty of it as well. We are a temple and need to care for self. Our bodies respond to how bad or how well we care for it. Commit today to making changes and share those changes.

List your changes. Remember, small steps. (Examples: I will cut soda out of my diet for the next two weeks. I will walk 15 minutes every morning. I will schedule my GYN appointment this month.)

_____

_____

_____

_____

_____

_____

_____

_____

Choose to listen and read things that are uplifting. Don't listen to breakup songs if you're going through a break up! If you are having a tough time focusing, ask your friends to create a playlist that is uplifting, and ask them to write verses or positive statements that you can see in the places that you frequent. List what songs you like to listen to or genre of music that is uplifting. List your favorite writers with positive statements.

List your favorite verses, songs, etc.

_____

_____

_____

_____

_____

_____

_____

_____

_____

_____

_____

_____

Pray. If you could tell God how you feel, no holds barred, what would you say? Go ahead and write it down here. Tell Him what's been on your heart.

_____

_____

_____

_____

_____

_____

_____

_____

_____

_____

_____

_____

_____

_____

What are you grateful for today, this moment? Can't think of anything? How about the roof over your head, the food on the table, being surrounded by people who love you or care?

List five things below that you are grateful for. Take it a step further. Each night before you go to bed, write five things that you are grateful for. It can be a person, pet, place or thing.

_____

_____

_____

_____

_____

_____

_____

_____

_____

_____

_____

_____

_____

Is there anything that has been circling in your mind that is keeping you up at night or that you are worried about? Write it all out here.

_____

_____

_____

_____

_____

_____

_____

_____

_____

_____

_____

_____

_____

_____

_____

_____

_____

_____

_____

_____

_____

_____

_____

_____

_____

_____

_____

_____

_____

_____

_____

_____

_____

_____

Journaling is one of the greatest gifts you can give to yourself. Journals are reminders of not only the bad but the good. It will remind you how you have been able to get dressed again and again. How you have been pulled out of certain circumstances and how God has come to your rescue. You need those reminders to become brave when things are dismal, to bring in hope when you feel helpless, and to place the timer on the situation that doesn't seem to end.

Each time you take the action to counteract something negative with a positive, you **GET DRESSED.** You embellish and accessorize your beautiful wardrobe made of strength and dignity. Don't quit. Don't lose hope. If you find you can't move forward, get help.

ξ EIGHT ξ

ξ

Choice Dresses

NO MATTER HOW PREPARED, organized and ready you think that you are, life has the potential to strip you. There were a few takeaways I had with my experience and I would like to highlight some for you.

Being my best advocate, especially when it comes to my health, is one of the best continual gift to self.

Control is an illusion. As much as I would like to think I am in control of everything, I have raised my white flag from time to time and have admitted that I am not.

Surrendered prayer and the invitation to keep God in all areas in life helps me keep balanced.

No matter how many times I am told that I am an incredible woman, I have to believe it; especially God's definition as His daughter.

The right expectations in my mind and the communication of the same will protect me from letting my mind go down the assumption path.

My faith will be tested. The foundation of my core beliefs will break or sustain me. I am expected to walk by faith.

My trust will be tested and with good reason. Usually it's in those times where I find new things about myself and God. To get back to

111

some type of normalcy requires one or more, okay…sometimes a lot of actions from me. Some of those actions I will not like. Others, I really need to do so that I can heal physically, emotionally and/or spiritually.

To **GET DRESSED** after life happens is a choice.

Each positive action you take, no matter how small they are, makes a difference. Each time you invite God to be part of any decision, it makes a difference. Just like your wardrobe has a variety of outfits you can dress in, your life is presented with the same as well. Often women miss the opportunity to get dressed into a nicer or more appropriate outfit. They have become comfortable with their old wardrobe, and continue to use their clothes until they become tattered or worn. We do the same in life.

Circumstances can strip you to the point where you need overhaul the wardrobe. It is presented as opportunities to change your outfits.

I call these outfits:

- New Choices
- New Decisions
- New Reactions

Notice, all of the outfits listed above have the word new before them. You cannot continue to outfit yourself with the old because after you go through the fire of pain, loss or illness, they are no longer useful. Those outfits can no longer be worn because you have been impacted negatively. The stench requires you to throw out the old and bring in the new.

Let's talk about your new future outfits.

> You will always be presented with choices. (Think of choices as colors.)

Your decisions (think of a dress) are based on your choices and that will create your outcome. (The outcome is to buy or not to buy.)

Your reactions (think of revealing or conservative) will determine both your choices and your decisions.

When you are faced with a decision, you are first presented with a choice, but your reaction influences whether your sway will be towards the choice to make bad or good decisions.

After all I had been through, I had the choice to be mad at God or trust Him. I made the decision to trust Him because after my short tantrum (bad reaction), I realized that He was not the cause of any of my pain. My negative reaction, in this case, was short-lived. When the next negative thing rolled around, my reaction was to think positive and trust God.

There will be times where you have to train yourself to have no reaction, a neutral one or something that is contrary to your personality and nature. (You know the inner gal you have to shove down with your heel and say, down girl, down!)

Your choices, your decisions and your reactions have the potential to strip you or dress you, again and again. As long as we are on this earth, it will happen. This means that you have to be proactive and fully engaged in order to stay fully dressed and armored up, for the most part.

There is a secret though that I must share with you about the whole getting dressed exercise. When you decide to put on that beautiful, positive-dress, it only becomes permanent when God is the one who partners with you during the shopping spree. Why? Because He will always help you pick something that is high-end, well-made and has eternal value.

We share stories because we can't help but be moved by love when we hear about pain and suffering. It is in our spiritual nature within our human experience. Sharing this story with you and many others has been an incredible, learning journey for me.

The permission to share a going-through story is not a ticket to dwell. It should be from the vantage to encourage empathy, understanding and compassion. It should be the hand on the shoulder that says it's okay. It should also be the encouragement that resounds loudly like a blowing whistle of a train upon departure with the assurance that there may be hard days ahead but a destination will be reached.

I've been told countless times that I am a strong woman. I readily admit that I didn't feel like one when all these things piled up on me. Here's something all women should know. Never go by feelings. They are fickle and change like undies. When stuff happens and they will happen, you have to remind yourself that the state of being stripped is temporary. You have to **GET DRESSED**!

Self-Evaluation

ξ

Dressed for Transparency

ONE OF THE THINGS THAT STAND OUT FOR ME after this part of my journey was the importance of transparency. I cannot begin to explain to you how it impacted the women in my church when I began to share bits and pieces of my journal. It helped them understand that someone like me really understands what some of them go through because we've been there, done that or have experienced something similar, if not the same.

For me, transparency does not mean that I divulge everything to everyone. It means that sometimes it's okay not to give the pretense of always feeling great so that vulnerability is shared. In my case, I used it as a way to teach my girls that there are times where they will be faced with tough decisions, deep hurts or losses but they will always find a place of comfort in Almighty God; if they choose to believe. (By the way, did I mention I love my women's group dearly?)

How often do you, as woman, pretend that all is okay in your world? You are expected to keep it together at all cost. The problem is that the cost is you. Women constantly put themselves last. They make their appointments last or not at all. They eat last or poorly. Women usually do not keep up with their health or overall wellness. When they do, in most cases, it's because they had a rude wake up call.

One of the greatest things we have learned within my staff is to allow any of us to be able to say no without condemnation. This doesn't apply to just things that need to be done to run the ministry, but personal things as friends. Women tend to guilt one another into doing things even if the other is overloaded. For some reason, we condone busyness. We're women, we can handle it right?

Unfortunately, that attitude does not allow a woman to say, "No, I can't or it's too much", without the snicker or frown from another.

On my team, we have established the freedom to say "No." Transparency encourages freedom without conditions. It brings the comfort of knowing that others are in the same boat, and it helps them breathe easier instead of feeling like they're the only ones in turmoil.

What are some areas where you pretend? Why?

_____

_____

_____

_____

_____

_____

_____

_____

_____

_____

_____

_____

A few months after my hysterectomy, one of the gals asked me, how are you? Before I could catch myself, I told her I was overwhelmed with sadness because in a period of three days, two close friends were diagnosed with cancer, Stages III and IV respectively, and it was a bit too much for me at the moment. My emotions were raw. She was taken aback. I am usually all smiles but that day I couldn't get it together. I was still processing. She looked at me and said, you've never said something like that to me before. My response back to her was that maybe I should do that once in a while.

YOUR *Transparency Plan*

You need to be real. Things are not always great. There are times when curve balls come and life sucks. Now don't take this as an excuse to do the pity party thing for days, months or years on end. It also doesn't mean that you rehearse your story with everyone you encounter or retell it over and over again. Transparency is when you share to edify or build others up. It is not so that you can feel better, get attention or play victim.

There is also a flip side. Some women will not share their story because they do not trust anyone; they don't trust the reaction; or they have been taught to keep it to themselves. It's nobody's business. I agree that certain things should not be shared or only shared with trusted friends. However, there are some stories and experiences that other women need to hear because it will free them and empower them to become better, to heal and to move forward.

Do you have a story like that? Write it here.

_____

_____

_____

_____

GET DRESSED with a shared story of transparency and love with the intention to build others. This is one of the greatest gifts you can give someone, stranger or friend. One of the greatest gifts Jesus gave to his 12 closest friends was his transparency. They saw Him act in love, cry, get angry, experience fear, go through agony and finish in triumph. It helped them accept forgiveness, be courageous and accomplish their life calling, which I may add cost most of them their lives.

It's my prayer that you share those stories that will help another get through. Bless them with your transparency.

Today...

It didn't take me long to throw back on some new outfits because imbedded are strengths that can never be taken away...shaken, perhaps, but never taken. My strengths were inherited because of my upbringing, my experiences and most importantly, because of my God.

> I hope these words brought you comfort if you're going through. Please know that you're not alone. We all go through.

> I hope these words bring you preparedness for your next opposition.

> And... I hope that these words bring you compassion for those who are experiencing adverse circumstances and have need of you.

Remember, just because you were temporarily stripped, doesn't mean that you have to remain that way. Learn, grow and outfit yourself again. **GET DRESSED!**

About the Author

Roz Humphreys is an author and motivational speaker. For over 30 years, Roz has encouraged women of all ages to recognize their value and potential. Her no-nonsense attitude laced with Latin love, has steered and encouraged women towards wholeness. Her educational resources and women's forums continue to motivate women to pursue their passion and purpose.

Roz is the Director over the women's ministry in Faith Church, a megachurch in the Northeast, located in western Connecticut. Roz and her husband Richard are native New Yorkers who have embraced New England's beauty and charm. They have 2 young adult daughters.

How can I be so optimistic? I believe that God is the painter of my masterpiece life. The end of His book tells me that my painting, my life, has a promised and beautiful outcome; eternity. It would be unfair not to invite you to have the same faith and the same hope.

Do you know Jesus?

God sent His only son as a gift of reconciliation for you. All God has ever wanted is relationship. Through His son Jesus Christ, He has offered salvation and an eternity with Him in heaven. The greatest offer on earth is dependent on your acceptance. God will never impose on your free will.

If you would like to accept Jesus as your Savior, say the following prayer, email me and let me know!

> Jesus, come into my life. Forgive me of my sins. I accept you as Lord and Savior.

Find yourself a bible-believing church in your area and learn more about living life for God as soon as possible.

If this book has changed your life or provided insight, make sure you tell a friend or two and when you have time, let me know too!

Bunches of blessings to you and I hope to hear from you soon.

getdressedbook@gmail.com

Holding Your Arms Up

In Exodus 17, Israel was in a battle against the Amalekites. As long as Moses held up his arms, the Israelites were on the winning side. During the battle, Moses' arms began to tire so Aaron and Hur came alongside him and kept his arms up.

Sometimes in life, we have to come alongside someone who is battling to give them hope and courage to continue in their fight until it is won.

The Story Behind the Book

Many people wonder what was the motivation or inspiration behind a book.

This was never meant to be a book. Well at least not for me! This was an obedience journey. It was my challenge from God to be transparent; to be real with others. Often what is shared is limited because people have a tendency of putting those in leadership on pedestals. People who are in leadership have struggles just like you. The only difference is that they have greater responsibilities in certain areas and were courageous enough to live out their destiny or calling. To live by example is a tough place to be at and yet each and every one of us has been called to do just that. We are called to be an example of Jesus by living a life that exudes love.

I answered the call to transparency because I noticed the huge gap that there is when people say, "I went through this" and then end it with "but praise God, I have the victory." No one wants to discuss the stuff in the middle. It makes Christianity seem like something that is mystical and that is only available to the saintly few. It makes life look like a cake walk when it truly isn't at times. There's a boat load of pain in this world, and we have been summoned to heal the hurting. If someone cannot relate with you, they cannot be healed through you.

Stories should include what people want to hear. They want to know how you really felt. They want to know the struggles you went through and the questions that bombarded your mind. They want to be assured that doubts and fear are going to come, but they also want to welcome the steps you took to get past it. Sharing emotions is huge. Anyone can relate. Emotions have a universal language.

Although this book wasn't a planned intention in my heart at first, it was certainly a planned and a very intentional one in God's. It eventually became a purposeful share that changed me in a profound way. I saw the impact it had even before it was published.

You have been waiting on the other side of my obedience for this book. Thank you for being part of my journey and my motivation.

Coming Soon...

STOP IGNORING ME...The Cry of My Heart

If the woman inside of you could get your attention for one moment, what would she ask? What does she crave, wish, hope and pray for? Would you be willing to listen intently and lovingly? Think about it, if you can't treat yourself lovingly and with intention, how are you going to be your best for others?

Too many of us have chosen to ignore ourselves and our dreams because we are overwhelmed with our other roles and the demands life has placed on us. We neglect our needs and wear our neglect as a badge of sacrifice. Unfortunately, that badge eventually sticks its needle right into the most precious part of our being; our heart. There is no escaping this. If you have not yet felt the piercing pain of neglect, it will happen sooner than later.

Stop Ignoring ME was designed to purposely guide you through a must-take journey that will help you get the type of life you've desired for so long. You will learn how to be kind to yourself...first. Kindness to self is one of the key factors to experience healing. Why is that so important? Your healing process cannot start, proceed, or continue until your kindness focus becomes a priority in your life. It requires a lot of work, and the work will be worth it because, at the end of the journey, you will find inner-peace and true fulfillment in order to live the life you have always desired.

If you would like to know of future books, join our mailing list. Send an email to rozreaders@gmail.com.

References

Chapter 5
Steve & Sarah Berger, Have Heart: Bridging the Gulf Between Heaven and Earth (Tennessee/Grace Chapel, Inc., 2010), 66.

33267808R00081

Made in the USA
Middletown, DE
06 July 2016